BIRMINGHAM RAILWAY CARRIAGE & WAGON COMPANY

A CENTURY OF ACHIEVEMENT
1855-1963
IN PICTURES AND WORDS

John Hypher, Colin and Stephen Wheeler

BRC&W built up a sizeable fleet of wagons for rental. Many of these carried the company name as depicted by this 8 ton example which was built around the turn of the century.

© J. Hypher, C. Wheeler, S. Wheeler and Runpast Publishing, September 1995

Typesetting and reproduction by Viners Wood Associates, Painswick, Glos.
Printed by The Amadeus Press Ltd, Huddersfield.

ISBN 1 870754 34 4

Introduction

The Birmingham Railway Carriage & Wagon Company started life as the Birmingham Wagon Company in 1854. From small beginnings of hiring-out and selling wagons, BRC&W progressed to manufacturing not only wagons but also coaches. Expansion ensued at a good pace and the company became a well respected and major supplier to both home and overseas railways. During the first world war, the workshops were turned over to producing armoured trucks, shells and aircraft for the fighting services. Rolling stock ranging from Pullman cars and special luxury coaches to small freight wagons were produced and went on to include diesel railcars and electric multiple units. Buses and trolleybuses were also built before the second world war and at the commencement of hostilities, the works were again called upon to make implements of war. These included scout cars, tanks, aircraft parts and large transport gliders. The post-war years once again saw BRC&W producing rolling stock for both Britain and overseas. Apart from carriages and wagons, diesel and electric multiple units and railcars, diesel-electric locomotives were produced for export to Australia, Africa and Eire as well as in good quantities for British Railways. With excess capacity in the industry and with vastly reduced orders being placed by operators, BRC&W closed its gates for the last time in 1963.

This book is not intended to be a definitive history of the Birmingham Railway Carriage & Wagon Company, but rather, as the title suggests, a reflection of a century of achievement. The text and illustrations are designed to give a flavour of the Company's activities, markets, customers and products, rather than a comprehensive account of everything that left the factory.

All photographs and drawings are from the private collections of Colin and Stephen Wheeler and of John Watkins, unless otherwise credited.

Acknowledgements

We acknowledge with grateful thanks the help given to us by the following people and organisations in supplying information, photographs, or both for inclusion in this book.

Albert Williams, Brian Colley, William Murphy, Jorge L San-Martin, Terry Rawlins (Tearne and Sons), Stafford Records Office, Sulzer Diesel, T Timmins, Malcolm Keeley, Bob Greenaway, the National Railway Museum, and J C Gillham.

Special thanks go to Terry Bye, John Watkins and J H Price for making their collections of material on BRC&W freely available to us.

John Hypher, Colin Wheeler and Stephen Wheeler
May 1995

Contents

Aerial view of the BRC&W plant.

4

CHAPTER 1

Enterprise and Growth

Well over a century has now elapsed since a group of Birmingham businessmen got together to seize the opportunities afforded by the railway mania which was sweeping the country. They saw a lucrative market in supplying wagons by both hiring them out and providing them on a hire-purchase basis as well as selling them outright.

An Act of Parliament had been passed in 1845 which allowed the use of privately sponsored mineral and coal wagons to run on the railways and facilitated the availability of lower charges to be made. The introduction of privately owned wagons came much to the relief of the railway companies whose own stock was unable to cope with demand due to the volume of traffic being transferred from the canals and roads.

Accordingly, the Birmingham Wagon Company came into being on 29 December 1854, its objects being to finance collieries, coal merchants and other traders to enable them to possess their own railway wagons which the company would provide, maintain and repair for an appropriate fee.

It was registered on 20 March 1855 and became a limited company the following year. The initial board of directors heading this pioneering venture were Benjamin Goode, Benjamin Dain, Joseph Jennens, Richard Cookson, William Nicks and John Goode. Some of these gentlemen were Freemasons which may have accounted for the five pointed Masonic emblem being adopted as the company symbol.

Based originally at 101 New Street, Birmingham, the company later re-located to Newhall Street. Before going into manufacturing itself, wagons were made and maintained on behalf of the Birmingham company by Brown, Marshall and Company of Saltley. This arrangement lasted for nine years, but it was projected that the Saltley firm would be unable to supply sufficient wagons to meet the ever increasing demand and the company made arrangements to secure its own premises at Smethwick.

This was master-minded by Edmund Fowler, a former LNWR goods clerk, who had been appointed as manager and secretary of the Birmingham Wagon

A covered wagon from the rental fleet seen outside the works around the turn of the century.

Private owner wagons became quite prolific. This steel bodied, 20 ton wagon was built in 1909 for Brymbo and bears a Great Western Railway registration plate on its frame.

Vacuum Oil Co. 10 ton tanker built in 1910. Note the ornate BRC&W plate centrally placed above the frame.

Brake 3rd coach No.12 supplied to the Highland Railway Company in 1896.

PHOTO: Brian Yates.

7

Company. His business acumen built the company into a successful market leader from its small beginnings on ten acres of farmland alongside the Great Western Railway. In 1864 the first plant was constructed and a modest weekly output of four wagons was initially achieved.

An annual assessment was made of outstanding monies owed by customers and in 1869, for instance, a total of £2145.10s.9d was owed by a spread of 19 companies.

A programme of continuous expansion saw both the company and its range of products increase and 1876 saw the construction of its first passenger coaches. As horse trams came on stream up and down the country, the company entered that market too and supplied examples to the transport undertakings of several towns and cities from the early 1880s.

In 1878, the company decided that its diverse portfolio of rail-borne products was no longer reflected in its trading name and consequently changed it to the Birmingham Railway Carriage & Wagon Company. Within about three decades of inauguration the BRC&W, now producing about 50 wagons a week, was a significant builder of rolling stock not only for the home market but also for developing overseas railways. Many of the British Colonies were among the growing and impressive list of world-wide customers. Indeed, it is said that some of the company's directors played a part in running British owned railways in Argentina.

Smethwick Works Football Club was started during the 1880s and its playing field called 'Stony Oval' was located on the present site of Sydenham Road. With over one thousand men to choose from, it was hardly surprising that it became one of the best teams in the area and, in 1890, won the Birmingham Junior Cup. Continuing development meant sacrificing 'Stony Oval' but another pitch was found on an area of land now known as Lewisham Park. The Earl of Dartmouth had leased this to the local council for a nominal rental but in 1899 the players were on the move yet again, this time to the Harry Mitchell Park. Perhaps predictably, they had to move once more but shortly afterwards the team was disbanded and the never-ending search for further pitches became unnecessary.

Their most notable player had been William 'Nigger' Newall, who apart from being an outstanding footballer was equally noted for his black curly locks! He went on to play for West Bromwich Albion and the club secretary later became a director of Albion.

Meanwhile, BRC&W's manager, Edmund Fowler, had been appointed as managing director and had a house built on the corner of Middlemore Road which he called 'The Laurels'. It was an extensive property and in the adjoining field he kept a cow which provided the household with fresh milk! A true Victorian gentleman, Mr Fowler maintained a keen interest in the company's activities until his death on 27 May 1904. 'The Laurels' was eventually demolished in 1967 and its place taken by a filling station.

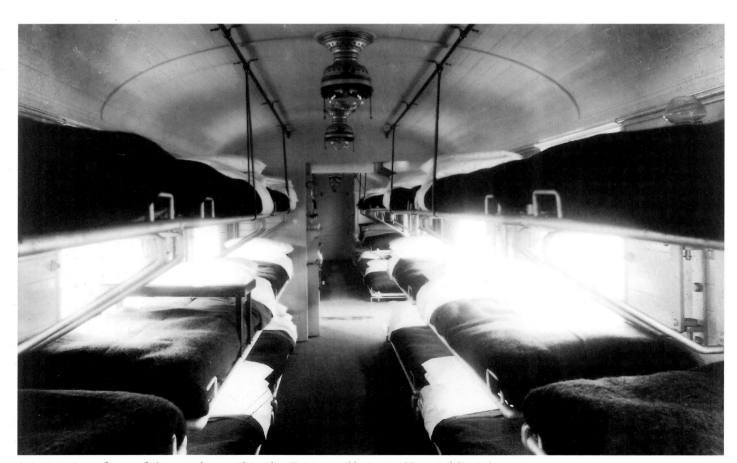

Interior view of one of the coaches within the 'Princess Christian Hospital Train'.

Part of the seven-coach 'Princess Christian Hospital Train' which was built in 1898 for service in South Africa during the Boer War. This was the world's first hospital train which was regrettably short-lived, as it was destroyed by the Boers.

BRC&W pulled out all the stops during the opening stages of the South African war. A 7-coach hospital train – the first ever – was built in 1898 for service in this extensive and war-torn country. Full mobile hospital facilities were required to be moved quickly to where they were most needed and this train, the 'Princess Christian Hospital Train', met this need. Of wooden construction, accommodation for both patients and staff was provided together with operating rooms, a dispensary and a kitchen.

Having built the complete train, it was then dismantled and shipped to South Africa in c.k.d. form (completely knocked down). The entire operation was achieved in just eleven weeks and upon arrival it was reconstructed again in Durban. Princess Christian, after whom the train had been named, visited the company's works at Smethwick on 22 December 1898 whilst it was under construction and described it as 'a stupendous piece of work in so short a time'. Hospital trains have since become a familiar and essential piece of kit during times of war. The honour fell to this particular train to be the first to enter the town of Ladysmith following liberation from the Boer siege. A former BRC&W employee who had joined the army was posted for action in South Africa and during his service there beheld a familiar sight in the shape of this train which he had helped build! Regrettably, it later became a war casualty after being torched by the Boers. Its Red Cross ownership did not prevent its destruction, as the Boers had convinced themselves that it was carrying arms and ammunition rather than the wounded and medical staff.

Just after the turn of the century, BRC&W started supplying the underground railways in the capital. This began in 1903 with deliveries to the Central London Railway which later became part of the London Underground network. The order comprised forty, 42-seater motor cars bearing CLR numbers 229 to 268; each being powered by two traction motors. Another landmark was achieved by the company when it produced the first all-steel passenger coaches in this country. These were built in 1904 for the Central London Railway also and consisted of six control trailers, which like the previous order, were constructed to tube specifications.

Wagon production still accounted for a significant proportion of output, but in the main were now being sold to the various railway companies rather than rented. Many of those which were rented out however, carried either the BRC&W company name or owners plates on them, but these arrangements came to a conclusion during the 1930s.

Overseas orders for wagons and coaches continued to flood in from new and existing satisfied customers. This enabled BRC&W to maintain a leading position in rolling stock construction. Wagons of every description and purpose were built, which included those for carrying wood, steel, minerals, cattle and general merchandise among others. Their destinations included such places as Argentina, Sudan, Manchuria, India and Chile while passenger coaches left our shores for Malaya, Argentina and Chile.

Weedon Bros leased this 1912 8 ton coke wagon from new. The star symbol at the front and the large oval plate on the side reveal that BRC&W is the owner.

This 4 wheel, 10 ton open wagon was built for the Great Central Railway in 1904. Note the tarpaulin rail.

The Great Central Railway also took delivery of this huge steel bodied, 40 ton, bogied loco coal wagon in 1904.

This delightful horse box was ordered by Frank Bibby and was based at the famous equestrian town of Newmarket. Delivered in 1911, it was fitted for air braking, vacuum braking and steam heating.

Hopton-Wood Stone certainly believed in eye-catching lettering for their 1911 5 plank 10 ton open wagon photographed before delivery. This was part of the BRC&W rental fleet.

A 6-plank, 10 ton 4-wheel wagon dating from 1911. Note the unusual hinged door flap.

Stubbs & Company were the owners of this 1912 salt wagon. It is fitted with a tarpaulin rail. Stafford Common station, shown as the wagon's home, was on an isolated Great Northern Railway branch from Broomshall Junction near Uttoxeter.

3-plank 10 ton open wagon produced for the North Staffordshire Railway in 1912.

1912 10 ton covered goods wagon supplied to the London and North Western Railway.

Another wagon from the rental fleet is this unusual pitched roof covered wagon, which was assigned to Chance & Hunt in 1913. This firm operated chemical works.

GALATEA. One of the two Pullman cars to be supplied to the Metropolitan Railway in 1910. These were among the first Pullman's to be built by BRC&W.

1910 saw a new chapter in the company's life begin. Indeed, it was in this year that BRC&W started building Pullman cars. Among the first were umber and cream liveried *MAYFLOWER* and *GALATEA* for the Metropolitan Railway. These two Kitchen Parlour Cars were to remain the only examples to be used by London Transport and its predecessors. They ran exclusively between Aylesbury and Liverpool Street from June 1910 until October 1939 (but not during the first world war), providing accommodation for 19 passengers and including a bar, toilet and heating. Dimensionally, these were 59ft 7ins long, 8ft 4ins wide over body panels and 12ft 3ins high.

A further ten cars were built during the year for service with the South Eastern and Chatham Railway, with another example being completed the following year. These were:

Parlour Cars (24 seats) – *SORRENTO CORUNNA SAVONA SAPPHIRE PALERMO*
Kitchen Parlour Cars (19 seats) – *VALENCIA FLORENCE CLEMENTINA EMERALD REGINA*
Non-supplement Kitchen Dining Car (1911) (24 seats) – *SHAMROCK*

These cars were delivered to the South Eastern and Chatham Railway in crimson lake livery and cost £5000 each.

A special and luxurious coach measuring some 78 feet in length was also built for the President of Argentina. Entry was gained by a grandiose central doorway and once inside, the three bedrooms, two bathrooms, day saloon, study and attendants room were accessed by side corridors.

A major BRC&W customer for a number of years was Argentina and in 1910 Buenos Aires held a rolling stock Grand Prix which the company won. Indeed, it had already supplied 70% of this region's operating stock. In 1911 the Buenos Aires Pacific Railway awarded a slightly unusual contract to the company for the supply of 1000 wagon axle boxes and 100 wagons without either wheels or axles. Further orders were later received for another 365 wagons without running gear. On the home front, the Great Western Railway called for 1000 iron framed ten ton open goods wagons in 1911, while other freight orders around this time came from the London and North Western and the North Staffordshire Railways.

Then in 1912 for something completely different, the company received orders for the manufacture of street-lights and bank safes(!) – the former being for local use by Birmingham Council and the latter for internal use with BRC&W's own banking and finance subsidiary.

In 1913, the Central Argentine Railway took delivery of three self-contained and luxurious family saloons, which can best be described as hotels on wheels. Measuring 10ft 6ins wide by 71ft 4ins long and 13ft 3ins high, they were corridored throughout. Each ran on a pair of 5ft 6in gauge, six wheel bogies and were finished externally in teak. At one end of the coach an

The South Eastern and Chatham Railway had their Pullman cars delivered in crimson lake livery. Kitchen Parlour Car *FLORENCE* is seen after completion in 1910.

Parlour Car *CORUNNA* was also constructed in 1910 and painted in crimson lake livery for use on the South Eastern and Chatham Railway.

Special coach built for the use of senior managers of the Buenos Aires Pacific Railway around the turn of the century.

First class coach No.101 constructed in 1904 for the Buenos Aires Pacific Railway.

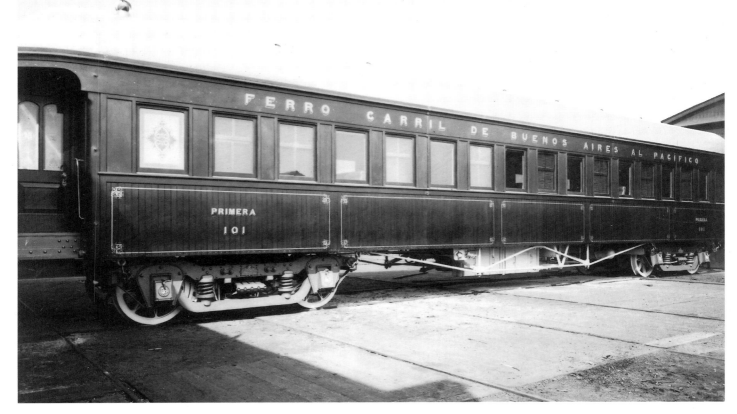

BRC&W won the 1910 Buenos Aires rolling stock Grand Prix. This advertisement leaves the would-be customer in no doubt as to what the company can supply.

observation saloon, complete with a coal fireplace, was luxuriously fitted-out and boasted not only an early form of hot water central heating but also electric ventilation fans. Three well appointed bedrooms were also featured, two of these containing 4 berths and the other, 2 berths. Their wash basins were fitted with both a hot and cold water supply and each bedroom was also provided with its own toilet. A lavish and well equipped ladies boudoir was also included as were two bathrooms – one for ladies and the other for gentlemen. The attendants compartment and heating chamber were situated at the far end of the coach. Saloon heating and hot water was provided by means of a coal fired slow combustion stove and furnace.

Labour unrest however was on the horizon in 1913 with the work-force seeking higher wages and trade union recognition. A series of strikes ensued among firms in the Midlands including BRC&W. Settlements with employers were agreed individually, but one success led to pressure elsewhere where conditions remained unchanged and where trade unionism was being resisted. Inevitably the spotlight eventually fell on BRC&W and its own troubles began with the night-shift on Friday 26 April. Strike action swept the

company and by the Monday a total walk-out stopped all production. This had been the first strike for forty years and despite negotiations taking place, no progress was made. BRC&W declared that they were paying standard wages for the work done by their employees and that any increase was out of the question. All 2000 workers were affected by this industrial action but within a few weeks workers from other rolling stock builders at Saltley, Oldbury and Wednesbury struck in sympathy. Some 30,000 workers, including a knock-on effect to allied trades and suppliers, were now affected.

A distress fund was opened for workers which provided dinners and a familiar sight was a cart being trundled along to bakers, greengrocers and butchers to obtain donated food. In an effort to evoke public support, the workers staged a hunger march from Smethwick to Liverpool and back. It took 16 days to cover the 280 mile round trip and only one person dropped out! By now the dispute had reached national level but after eleven weeks, a settlement was finally worked out between the respective managements and unions which significantly increased the wages of their workforces.

This composite coach was built in 1911 for the London, Tilbury and Southend Railway. It may have been used on the prestige service from St Pancras to Southend. In 1912 the LT&SR was taken over by the Midland Railway, the coach being renumbered to 3127, later becoming 4785 in LMS days. It was withdrawn in September 1946.

War and Peace

With the onset of the 'Great War', BRC&W played a prominent part in the war effort with much of its capacity being turned over to this very different type of production.

During the war years exports virtually ceased, other than for a small quantity of wagons bound for both South America and India during the opening year together with an order for France for 1000 open goods wagons.

Not unnaturally, it was the War Office which started the ball rolling with a substantial order for 2,300 wagons together with 200 brake blocks and 3,300 rifle clips. Other early orders from different sources comprised one for an 8-coach hospital train and another for 1350 ammunition wagons, the latter being placed by Vickers.

Five crimson lake liveried Pullman cars were delivered to the South Eastern and Chatham Railway during the early months of 1914, these being:-

Kitchen Parlour Cars (19 seats) *RUBY DAPHNE HAWTHORN MIMOSA*

and Parlour Car (24 seat) *TOPAZ*

The supply of munitions comprised a significant part of BRC&W's output, with an order for 25,000 4.5 inch high explosive shells being such an example, and placed during the summer of 1915. This was followed during October by a weekly order for 2000 shell forgings which was almost immediately increased to 5,300 per week. Hutments, armoured trucks, pontoons and even flag poles were also constructed for use during the war and an order for 500 Lewis machine gun tripod field mountings was also secured before BRC&W turned its attentions to the field of aviation.

Some company-owned land situated on the other side of Middlemore Road was put to use as an airfield in 1917 and equipped with a large hangar. The purpose of this was to accommodate both Handley Page and de Havilland aircraft which the company had been contracted to build. Local stories have it that the wingspan of the Handley Page 0/400 bomber was such that the wings are said to have had to be folded before they could enter or leave the hangar! This was reputedly the worlds' first multi-engined heavy bomber and although 120 of these bi-planes were ordered, it is

Another Pullman car for the South Eastern and Chatham Railway. *MIMOSA*, built during 1914 carries crimson lake colours. It is a Kitchen Parlour Car.

One of the large Handley Page heavy bombers which was built by BRC&W towards the end of the war.

Although 100 of these de Havilland DH10s were ordered, only a few were completed before hostilities ceased. One of those constructed by BRC&W is pictured.

believed that 93 were in fact built at Smethwick before hostilities ended. 100 de Havilland DH10 'Amiens' bomber aircraft were also ordered and allotted RAF numbers E6037-E6136. But it is thought that very few of these twin-engined bi-planes were actually completed before the conclusion of the war. Unlike today's aircraft, the wings of both these types were wooden framed and covered with fabric which was then 'doped', many local girls being employed on these tasks.

The report of the 65th Annual General Meeting relating to 1918 recorded that the first bomber was completed on Good Friday of that year and that by November, 60 had been completed and had been used to bomb towns along the Rhine. It further added that a single example had been in action at Zeebrugge.

With the war at last over, things started getting back to normal again. Orders from both the home and overseas railway markets gained momentum once more and comprised a healthy mix of goods and passenger vehicles. Goods vehicles of many shapes, sizes and uses were ordered during the early post war years and included hopper wagons, coal wagons, brake vans, lowsided, highsided, open, covered and tank wagons among others in both 4-wheel and bogie configuration. Overseas customers included The Gold Coast, Nigeria, Mauritius, Uganda, South Africa, Ceylon and Uruguay. Additionally, several Indian railway companies were supplied between them with large quantities of stock.

And within our own shores, the British Wagon Company, the Great Eastern, Great Western, London and North Eastern and the London Midland and Scottish Railways were numbered among recipients of Birmingham freight vehicles. A noteworthy local order

to the works was that for 100, 12 ton coal wagons for Smethwick Gas works for delivery in 1924, while another order from nearby West Cannock colliery in 1925 called for double that quantity. Meanwhile, the rental fleet was increased substantially during 1923 with 500, 12 ton coal wagons being built and leased to the Great Central Railway together with a further 150 for use by Charrington, Dale and Co.

On the passenger front it was a similar story. The Barry Railway, South Eastern and Chatham, Southern, Great Eastern, London and North Eastern and the London Midland and Scottish Railways all restocked with quantities of 1st, 2nd and 3rd class coaches as well as brake vehicles, many of which were bogied. The London Electric Railway Company placed an order during 1923 for standard tube stock which later became known as 'pre 1938'. The initial order called for 35 all-steel trailers which were delivered in 1925 and numbered 865-899 and were augmented by a further 50 trailers numbered 900-949 which arrived in 1926. These had been preceded in 1922 by a 48-seat sample trailer car numbered 823.

Coaches built to overseas orders went to Nigeria, The Gold Coast, Palestine (all of which were 68ft 5in long), Uganda, Mauritius, Egypt and Sudan while a 1920 order for Buenos Aires Western Railway called for 35 motor coach bodies of which 20 were first class and 15 second. The Palestine order comprised ten 45 seat first class and nine 112 seat third class coaches together with two special saloons. These were delivered in 1922 and were numbered as follows :-

Special saloons – 97 & 98, 1st class coaches – 120 to 129, and 3rd class coaches – 320 to 328.

British Potash owned this 12 ton hopper wagon which was constructed in 1920. Note the ratchet device, used to operate the bottom opening door.

12 ton open wagon with tarpaulin rail, built for the Great Western Railway in 1921.

BRC&W constructed wagons of many different types for both the home and overseas markets. Illustrated is a 1921 brake van for the Great Eastern Railway.

1923 14 ton tank wagon.

1923 20 ton brake van for the London and North Eastern Railway, probably a pre-grouping design.

This 7 plank 12 ton open wagon forms part of BRC&W's rental fleet. Built in 1924, it is seen in the colours of Brentnall and Cleland.

Another member of the rental fleet is this 1925 12 ton steel open wagon seen on hire to Tarmac.

A 3 plank dropside open wagon of 1925 awaiting delivery to the London, Midland and Scottish Railway.

OE 6156 was the first of 57 bus bodies built for 'Midland Red'. Seating was provided for 29 passengers. Constructed in 1920, they were placed on Tillings-Stevens TS3 chassis. Note the speed limit of 12mph painted on the chassis.

Argentina again featured in the luxury stakes in 1923 when an order was placed by the Argentine Transandine Railway for a special 7-car train comprising 4 Pullman type cars, 1 dining car, 1 kitchen and baggage car and a separate baggage car. Bogies were specified for each of these. The Egyptian and Sudan Governments also placed an order the same year for a special luxury saloon.

The first post war Pullman cars emerged during 1920/21 and were:-
Parlour Cars (1920) 26 seats
  PADUA CALAIS MILAN
Kitchen Parlour Cars (1920) 16 seats
  PORTIA PALMYRA ROSALIND
Kitchen Parlour Cars (1921) 27 seats
  ALBION ALEXANDRA NEVADA ATLANTA COLUMBIA
Brake Parlour Cars (1921) 30 seats
  CAR No.40 THIRD CLASS
  CAR No.41 THIRD CLASS
Dining Cars (1921) 47 seats
  CAR No.42 THIRD CLASS
  CAR No.43 THIRD CLASS
  CAR No.44 THIRD CLASS
CALAIS AND MILAN, at least, were built for use on the South Eastern and Chatham Railway.

1920 heralded another landmark for BRC&W when it entered the bus bodying business. The Birmingham and Midland Motor Omnibus Company known as 'Midland Red' placed an order for 57 single deck bus bodies, all of which were placed onto Tilling Stevens chassis.

These comprised:-
OE 6156-75 1920 Tilling Stevens TS3
  BRCW Front Entrance 29 seats
OE 6186-97 1920 Tilling Stevens TS3
  BRCW Front Entrance 29 seats
OH 1198-99 1920 Tilling Stevens TS3
  BRCW Front Entrance 29 seats
OH 1213-19 1920 Tilling Stevens TS3
  BRCW Front Entrance 29 seats
OH 1235-36 1920 Tilling Stevens TS3
  BRCW Front Entrance 29 seats
This accounts for 43 of the bodies which were placed on these chassis from new and it is known that the remaining 14 were used for re-bodying some of the above as well as other vehicles of the same marque. Bodyswaps were very commonplace and it is assumed that the other 14 'chassisless' bodies were kept as a float until swapping commenced in earnest!

Further Pullman vehicles were delivered in March 1923 and were of the Guard Parlour Car variety seating 26 and usually placed at the end of trains. Their names were:-
  AURORA FLORA JUNO MONTANA.
These were followed in 1924 by:-
Kitchen Parlour Cars (22 seats)
  ROSAMUND AURELIA FINGALL
and in 1925 by:-
Kitchen Parlour Cars (22 seats)
  CYNTHIA ADRIAN IBIS
Parlour Cars
  HERMIONE LYDIA RAINBOW LEONA MINERVA
  NIOBE OCTAVIA PLATO

Pullman Parlour Car *MINERVA*, completed 1925.

An end view of Parlour Car *RAINBOW* in 1925.

However, barely was the paint dry when ten of these were sold and whisked away to Italy in October 1925 for use between Milan and Nice by CIWL (Compagnie Internationale Des Wagon Lits):-

Their names were replaced by number as follows:-
51 *(ADRIAN)* 52 *(IBIS)* 53 *(LEONA)* 54 *(HERMIONE)* 55 *(LYDIA)* 56 *(NIOBE)* 57 *(OCTAVIA)* 58 *(RAINBOW)* 59 *(PLATO)* 60 *(MINERVA)*

All except *HERMIONE* and *RAINBOW* (which went to Egypt) returned to the fold in 1928 whereupon three were rebuilt by BRC&W and five by the Midland Railway Carriage and Wagon Co. the same year. Details are placed in the table below.

Former Name	CIWL No.	Rebuilt by	Rebuilt to	Name after rebuild
ADRIAN	51	MRC&W	Kitchen Car	*ADRIAN*
IBIS	52	MRC&W	Kitchen Car	*IBIS*
LEONA	53	MRC&W	Kitchen Car	*PRINCESS ELIZABETH*
LYDIA	55	MRC&W	Kitchen Car	*LYDIA*
NIOBE	56	MRC&W	Parlour Car	*ONYX*
OCTAVIA	57	BRC&W	Kitchen Car	*DIAMOND*
PLATO	59	BRC&W	Kitchen Car	*PEARL*
MINERVA	60	BRC&W	Guards Parlour	*LADY DALZIEL*

Meanwhile, *HERMIONE* and *RAINBOW* were re-christened *KARNAK* and *CLEOPATRA* for service in Egypt.

BRC&W was commissioned to carry out six conversions involving kitchen cars during 1924. This comprised converting *ANSONIA* and *ARCADIA* into 16 seat first class Brake Parlour Cars, *CAR NO. 46 and 57 THIRD CLASS* into 18 seater Brake Parlour Cars and *CAR NO. 40 and 41 THIRD CLASS* into 30 seater Brake Parlour vehicles.

During May 1924 CIWL placed their first order with the company for 30 steel bodied dining cars together with a special 42 seat dining car (No.2700) for the French Presidential train. These were numbered 2852 -2881 and were delivered towards the end of 1925 and during 1926 for service in Europe. 1926 also saw 15, 24 seat first class cars delivered for service on the 'Fleche D'or' which were numbered 4001-4015. Further 1926 deliveries included four 21 seat Pullman saloons for use in Egypt, numbered 2914-2917 and fifteen sleeping cars for the continent numbered 2918-2932. The Egyptian cars received the following names :-

2914 *LUXOR*, 2915 *ASSUAN*, 2916 *FAYOUM* and 2917 *SIWA*.

A small, yet prestigious order from the Union of South Africa was received in September 1923 for three vehicles to be exhibited at the British Empire Exhibition at Wembley in 1924. These were a first class saloon, a dining car and a kitchen/staff car. These eventually left our shores for South Africa during February 1926 following renovation the previous year.

More Pullman cars were produced during 1926 as follows:-

Kitchen Parlour Cars (46 seats)
CAR NO. 31 THIRD CLASS
CAR NO. 32 THIRD CLASS
CAR NO. 33 THIRD CLASS
Parlour Cars (54 seats)
CAR NO. 34 THIRD CLASS
CAR NO. 35 THIRD CLASS
CAR NO. 36 THIRD CLASS

Originally constructed by Clayton Wagons of Lincoln in 1920 as a Kitchen Parlour Car, *ARCADIA* was remodelled by BRC&W into a Brake Parlour Car during 1924. It is pictured following completion.

A further 4 cars were also delivered in 1926 to the Great Southern Railway of Ireland for use on their 5ft 3in gauge system. These were 46 seat Kitchen Parlour Cars and were numbered *CAR NO. 100 THIRD CLASS* to *CAR NO. 103 THIRD CLASS*. They measured 65ft 11ins long, 8ft 11ins wide and 12ft 5ins high.

Central Argentine Railways placed two interesting orders in 1925 for delivery in 1927. The first called for 600 buffer heads and shanks while the second was for seventeen first class trailers cars with motor car underframes, electrics, wheels and axles.

The final order of 1925 came from India and was for a special luxury saloon body for the Maharaja of Jodhpur which included teak, mahogany and walnut in its construction.

A peep into the Chairman's statements from 1919 to 1926 gives us an overview of the whole operation. At the end of 1918 half a million pounds worth of work was in progress and a trading profit of almost £107,500 was revealed for that year, which placed the Company in a sound financial position. Plans had been made before the war to extend the works but hostilities had prevented this being effected. However, at the time of the AGM in February 1920 this work was underway. The statements also reveal details of BRC&W's French connection.

It was decided that in order to carry out our contracts in France it would be of distinct value if we secured land and established a branch works there and during the past month I (Alfred Windle) in conjunction with your managing director went across to the works established at La Pallice, near La Rochelle and we were struck with the great possibilities of the value of these works. There are some 15 acres of ground which we secured alongside the railway and in very close proximity to the docks at La Pallice. These are so large that a boat of 20,000 tons lay alongside the quay and shortly these docks are to be brought right up to the edge of your works. If you have a doubt as to whether your money is safe there, I would remind you that during the past 12 months the value of the land at La Pallice has increased five or six times the amount we gave for it and I believe that the value of that port is so great that in all probability you will see a second Trafford Park at La Pallice. Arrangements have been made for the services of well-known French railway engineers to act as our agents on that side. And with the enormous amount of rolling stock that has to be replaced and cannot be replaced for very many years to come, the prospects of the country are distinctly good.

The report of directors in 1921 (67th AGM) stated that in spite of great hindrances and difficulties, most of which had been overcome, this works was achieving favourable progress. It was also explained that the French works was controlled by a separate company wholly owned by BRC&W.

Wagon repairs started again at Smethwick in 1920 after an absence of several years and some interesting details of dividends were also recorded which revealed a consistently healthy financial position for the Company. For 63 years BRC&W had paid an average of 11% but for the past 19 years this figure had held at 15%. It was pointed out that shareholders had received their capital back in 6 years.

At the 1922 AGM it was reported that the French

White liveried Pullman cars were operated in Egypt by C.I.W.L. One such car, No.2914 was named LUXOR. It is pictured in 1925 prior to shipping.

CAR NO 34 THIRD CLASS, was one of three similar third class Parlour Cars completed in 1926.

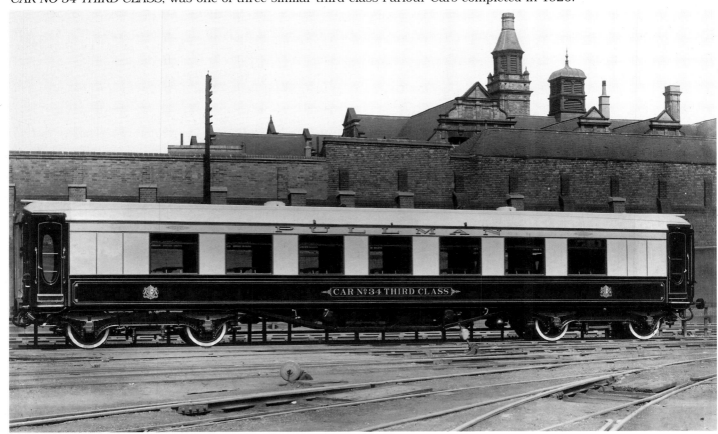

works had materially improved in value during the previous year and was also carrying out ship repairs.

The following year the chairman referred to an industrial dispute which closed the Smethwick works for a total of 6 weeks between March and June 1922. It would appear that the Company was not at the centre of the dispute but was a victim of it. The same year the north side extensions were completed and reference was made too, of many colonial orders being placed abroad, with the rate of exchange together with taxation making it impossible to compete with foreign factories. BRC&W provided a 15 acre recreation ground complete with pavilion and bandstand and facilities for football, cricket, tennis and bowls. This was run by the YMCA with the help of £100 per year from the Company.

1923 witnessed a downturn in the Company's fortunes with just a 6% dividend. Foreign competition with the added ingredient of low wages made the Company's products far more expensive by comparison. An example highlighted was of prices quoted for a South African order – BRC&W's price was £190,000 while a foreign competitor's bid was £147,000. Business at the works in La Pallice was described as dull.

There was good news and bad news at the 1926 AGM. The good news was that the extensions carried out on the north side of the works had been of inestimable value but the chairman's address painted a picture of commercial doom and gloom. Alfred Windle said:

It will be generally recognised that the past year has been one of great difficult and anxiety to those engaged in the rolling stock industry and particularly to those firms who are largely dependent on export orders. Competition has been exceedingly keen and while there has been a large amount of rolling stock enquired for, prices have not improved in spite of the increased demand. Continental manufacturers who formerly confined their attention to the supply of carriages and wagons in their own country have, owing to the dearth of such orders, sought to fresh fields. Being materially assisted by depreciated currencies, longer working hours and lower wages paid, they have succeeded in obtaining large orders formerly executed in this country. 43% of trade unionists in Germany work over 8 hours.

Things weren't any better at the French works either:

The greatly depreciated value of the Franc militates against any benefits from this source.

Much competition was reported in France because nearly all rolling stock came from Germany as reparations. However, some valuable orders from France had been secured.

C.I.W.L. sleeping car No. 2930 comprised part of the second order placed by this operator with BRC&W. 2930 entered service in 1926.

Pictured is a Southern Railway 8 ton cattle wagon thought to have been built during the 1930s. Possibly used for transporting prize-winning cattle, it is well appointed, with steam heating, also air and vacuum brakes, so was probably intended to run with passenger trains.

The same Southern Railway cattle wagon is shown with all apertures open.

CHAPTER 3

The Inter Years

Rolling stock of all kinds for service in many parts of the world kept the factory occupied during the twenties and thirties. Indeed, substantial orders for both bus and trolleybus bodies too were received from London Transport along with large orders for motorbus bodies from Birmingham Corporation. London Transport's faith in BRC&W quality was maintained with further orders for the Underground. Overseas customers included a number of Argentinian and Indian railways together with those in Bolivia, Kenya and Uganda, Brazil, Gold Coast, Egypt, Rhodesia, South Africa, Nigeria, Uruguay and Cuba.

Repeat orders from CIWL continued to come in as well as those for customers beyond Europe. Examples of the latter included 17 passenger coaches ordered in 1926 comprising a mix of 1st, 2nd and 3rd class vehicles for the Kenya and Uganda Railway, while Rhodesia Railways requirements were for 150 goods wagons. The following year CIWL took delivery of a further 25 cars numbered 4081-4085 for the 'Fleche D'or' and 4091-4110 for the 'North Star'. Those for the 'Fleche D'or' were 24 seat 1st class vehicles while the balance carried 38 passengers in 2nd class accommodation.

In our own capital, the District Line's 1927 K class surface stock started entering service in 1929. These were of all-steel construction and comprised 101 3rd class motor cars seating 40 with BT-H electro-magnetic control equipment and GEC WT54B traction motors. They were numbered between 499 and 699 but took only the odd numbers.

The Metropoliton Railway ordered 30 motor cars, 15 trailers and 10 control trailers in 1928 for delivery in 1930. This was 'T' class multiple unit stock which featured passenger compartments rather than the more usual seating arrangements.

They were numbered 9722-9731, 9776-9780 (trailers), 6712-6721 (control trailers) and 2712-2741 (motor cars).

Further arrivals of 'T' stock came during 1932/33 consisting of 18 motor cars (2742-2759), 33 trailers (9732-9745, 9781-9799) and 14 control trailers (6722-6735).

BRC&W also built containers. A 2.5 ton example for the Southern Railway is shown.

1926 three-compartment 20 ton tank wagon. One of the works' steam shunting locos, probably an Avonside 0-4-0 ST. No. 11, is glimpsed on the left.

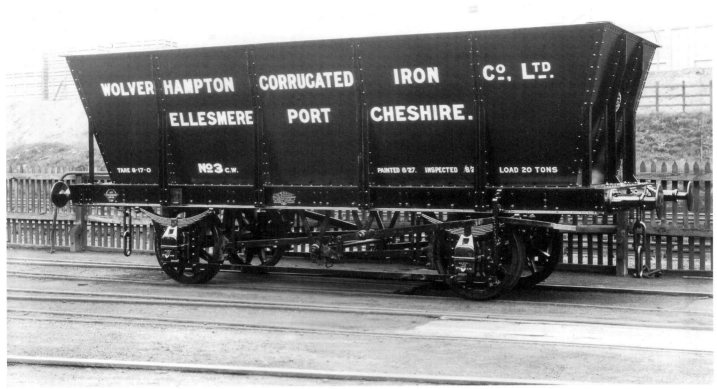

1927 20 ton steel bodied tippler wagon.

1928 20 ton steel bodied tippler wagon.

1928 20 ton hopper wagon.

20 ton hopper wagon produced for the Appleby Iron Company in 1929.

The London, Midland and Scottish Railway was the recipient of this impressive looking 40 ton bogied coal hopper which was completed in 1929. It has American style bogies.

Side view of the LMS 40 ton coal hopper showing the lines of this 1929 vehicle to advantage.

Full passenger brake van built for the LMS 1926. It was an experimental vehicle, given a vitreous enamelled steel body, and with unlined livery.

Full passenger brake van of a type built for the LMS between 1926 and 1930.

Vestibule brake/third coach produced for the LMS in 1926, one of a batch of 15 constructed by BRC&W.

1936 20 ton double bolster for the London, Midland and Scottish Railway.

1928 saw CIWL receive an additional 14 vehicles, all of which were for service in Egypt. These comprised numbers 3570-3577 which were 1st class sleeping cars together with 4171-4173 which were 1st class Pullman Kitchen Cars and 4174-4176, 1st class Pullman Parlour Cars seating 28. The Pullmans carried names as follows:-

4171 *EDFOU*, 4172 *BENDERA*, 4173 *ROSETTA*, 4174 *TUTANKAMEN*, 4175 *NEFERTARI* and 4176 *RAMESES*. Numbers 3570-3577 were built at a cost of £8,800 each while 4171-4176 were £6,850 each.

Nigerian Railways also ordered 140 25 ton high-sided bogie wagons at this time, while on our own shores the LMS received 50 brake vans.

1928 also saw neighbouring Metropolitan Carriage and Wagon Company sub-contract an order to BRC&W for the construction of 40 1st class bogie sleeping cars for CIWL. These comprised Nos 3416-3431 and 3432-3455, the latter being for service in Turkey. These entered service in 1929 at a cost of £9,105 each and were bought on a hire purchase basis. Similar arrangements also applied to 3570-7 and 4171-6

An interesting mixed bag of both bogied passenger and freight stock was required by the Great Western Railway of Brazil for delivery in 1929. These included 8 1st class coaches and a 1st class restaurant car together with 4 postal and baggage vans. The rest of

the order was made up of 44 25 ton covered goods wagons, 16 open wagons, 40 15 ton steel goods wagons and 6 12 ton timber cattle wagons making a grand total of 119 vehicles.

The same year (1929) saw BRC&W construct two 8-car articulated trains for the London and North Eastern Railway made up as follows:- one 3rd class/brake carriage, three 3rd class, two 1st/3rd class, one 2nd class and one brake carriage.

Rhodesia Railways, by comparison, called for a further 100 20 ton four wheel dropside wagons which saw delivery from early 1930. July 1929 produced the first order for diesel rail cars. Central Argentine Railways called for 10 70-foot vehicles which appear to have been used in service with trailers produced by the Yorkshire Wagon Company. BRC&W's motor cars provided capacity for 24 1st class passengers while the 2nd class trailers seated 54.

A substantial number of orders over the decades called for quantities of components or spares as opposed to complete vehicles. A few random examples are listed out of interest from the late 1920s:-

2500 Stones Patent lock hinges (home)
600 Buffer heads and shanks (export)
200 pressed steel bodyside plates (home)
2000 wheel centres, open spoke, unmachined (home)

DIAMOND started life named *OCTAVIA* in 1925. It was purchased almost immediately by C.I.W.L. for service in Italy and lost its name. It received the number 57 instead, until returning to the UK again in 1928. It was rebuilt as a Kitchen Parlour Car by BRC&W and renamed *DIAMOND*.

Interior of Pullman car No.4175 *NEFERTARI* which saw service in Egypt with C.I.W.L. This Parlour Car entered service in 1928.

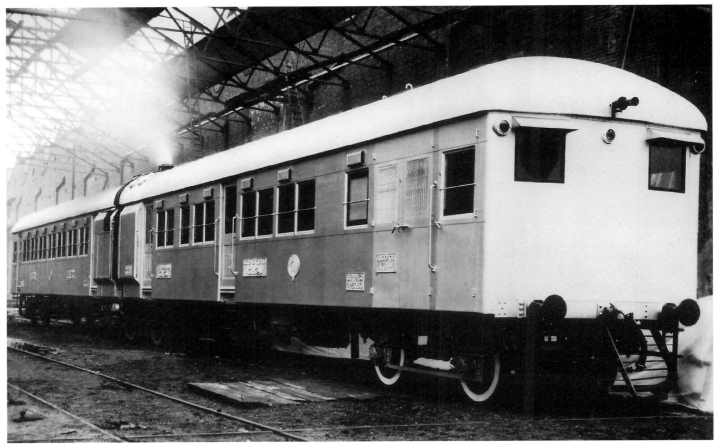

One of the steam powered twin articulated units built for Egypt during the early 1930s.

The new decade saw BRC&W producing its first steam rail cars for both Egypt and Argentina. Those for Egypt were 11 articulated double units, used for short passenger links and suburban workings, and at the time of their introduction were proclaimed as a 'notable advance'. An unusual feature of these units was the inclusion in the passenger accommodation of a second class Hareem compartment! There were also two single cars, used for conveyance of mails, perishable goods and animals. The steam power units were built by the Yorkshire Patent Steam Wagon Co of Hunslet, Leeds, of a type well tried in road vehicles. In March 1930, one of the articulated units worked a trial run between Wembley Park and Ayelsbury on the Metropolitan and Great Central Line. An experimental road/railcar was also constructed for use in Argentina. It was however, doomed never to see service and was converted for use as a waterside cafe!

1930/1 witnessed the entry into service of the last Pullman cars to be built by the company for another 20 years, until well after the war. These were 30-seat Kitchen Parlour Cars numbered 81 and 82 *THIRD CLASS* and 42-seat Parlour Cars numbered 83 and 84 *THIRD CLASS*. Still at home, 90 trailer cars numbered 7060-7149 were built for the Piccadilly line in 1931 to tube dimensions and were the last examples of standard tube stock to be built by the company. Another era came to an end in 1932 with the final batch of 25 *Compagnie Internationale des Wagons-Lits* cars leaving Smethwick. These sleeping cars were numbered 3743-3767.

But as one era came to an end another started – right on the doorstep. Birmingham Corporation Tramway & Omnibus Dept. took delivery of ten Daimler CP6 double deckers with BRC&W rear entrance 51 seat bodies during 1933. These carried fleet numbers 554 to 563 and were followed in 1934 by numbers 564 to 578 comprising Daimler COG5s with rear entrance 48 seat double deck bodies.

400 vacuum-braked 12 ton open wagons for the LMS were ordered in 1933, being followed by a repeat order during 1934.

During 1933, a Dorman engined petrol railcar was supplied to the Junagad State Railway and back home, 33 van bodies were constructed for the Royal Mail. Birmingham Corporation received a further 40 bus bodies constructed on Daimler COG5 chassis which entered service in 1935 with fleet numbers 634 to 673. Meanwhile, 100 bodies for London Transport's diesel engined AEC Q single deck chassis were ordered in 1934 for use in their country area, the first of these green liveried buses, classified 4Q4 by LT, being delivered in June 1935. These were 37 seaters and were given fleet numbers Q6-Q105. They were 27ft 5ins long, 7ft 6ins wide with an overall height of 9ft 1in. A further two were bodied by BRC&W in 1936 receiving fleet numbers Q186 and Q187.

1934 brought overseas orders for the construction of 16 3rd class sleepers for the Chinese Government Railway and a pair of diesel-electric rail cars for the 5ft 6in gauge Buenos Aires Western Railway.

These lightweight, streamlined, all metal railcars

A number of bus body contracts were completed for Birmingham Corporation Tramway & Omnibus Dept between 1933 and 1939. The first batch, of which this is one, were on petrol engined Daimler CP6 chassis. The remainder were Daimler COG5 models with Gardner 5LW diesel engines. Pictured is No.557 dating from 1933.   *PHOTO: Birmingham City Transport.*

1933 petrol driven railcar built for the Junagad State Railway, India. This metre gauge vehicle was powered by a Dorman engine.

BRC&W bodied a total of 102 of these side-engined AEC 'Q' chassis. Seating 37, these buses were used on country area duties. Q13 is pictured at Esher in April 1952. *PHOTO: J.C.GILLHAM*

Q77 in London Transport green livery is seen at Reigate. Built in 1936, this 37 seat AEC 'Q' still looks smart after 16 years of service. *PHOTO: J.C.GILLHAM*

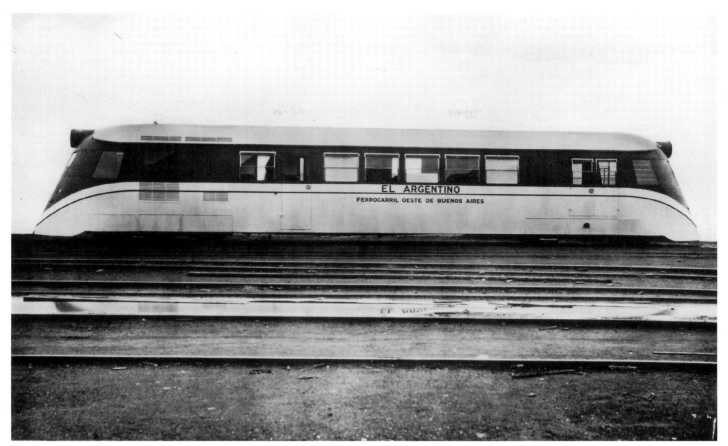

This diesel-electric railcar was produced in 1936 for the Buenos Aires Western Railway. It was powered by a Gardner 140hp engine and seated 20.

Plan and cutaway elevation of the 1936 diesel-electric railcars for the Buenos Aires Western Railway.

Additional Data

Main Generator Rating – 72kW, 400 amps, 650 volts	Overall Length – 57ft 4ins
Engine Rating – 140bhp @ 1100rpm	Width over body – 10ft 0ins
Weight in running order – 22 tons 16 cwt	Overall height – 9ft 11ins

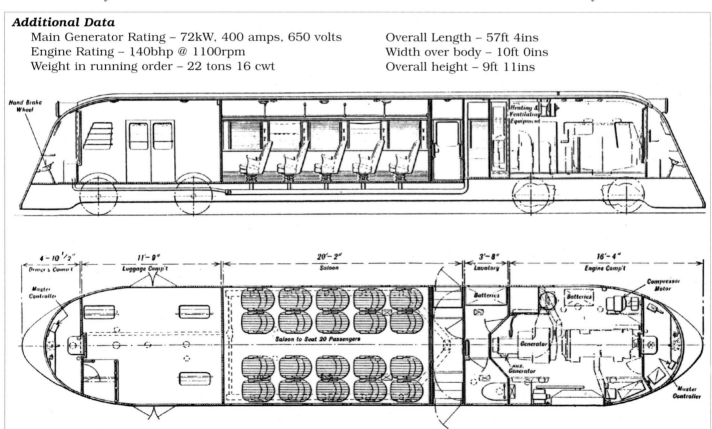

were delivered in 1936 and powered by a 6 cylinder 140 bhp Gardner L3 marine engine coupled to the main generator. Two 62hp Crompton Parkinson electric traction motors were situated in the bogie under the engine end of the car and a top speed of 65mph could be achieved. Seating for 20 passengers was provided and identical cabs were situated at each end of the vehicle.

New Year (1935) orders bode well for the Company's bus building activities with Birmingham Corporation starting the ball rolling with their requirement for 50 more double deckers. These, as with all future orders, were built on Daimler COG5 chassis upon which the undertaking had standardised. They were 54 seaters and were delivered the same year bearing numbers 744 to 793. This was followed by an order from Leyland for 30 trolleybus bodies to be fitted to their chassis for London Transport. These 60 seaters comprised the B1 class and were allocated LT fleet numbers 64-93 with deliveries commencing in November. A further 100 trolleybus bodies were ordered by London Transport for their AEC 664T chassis. Numbered 284-383, these 70 seaters became the C3 class and started to arrive in the capital in March 1936. Leyland again sub-contracted the trolleybus bodies for a further 70 chassis destined for London. These comprised sixty 70 seaters and ten 60 seaters. The seventy seaters which were delivered during 1937 were class D3 carrying fleet numbers 494-553 while the smaller vehicles delivered in September 1936 comprised five B1s numbered 489-493 and five B3s numbered 484-488. Birmingham rounded the year off just as they had started it with an order for another fifty buses which were completed by the end of the following year and numbered 794 to 843.

London trolleybus No.74 was part of the B1 class which started arriving in the Capital at the end of 1935. The 60 seat body is on a Leyland chassis.
PHOTO: J.C. GILLHAM

One hundred C3 class trolleybuses were built by BRC&W for service in London. No.309 was a 70 seater and was delivered during 1936. The 6-wheel chassis was an AEC 664T.
PHOTO: J.C. GILLHAM

Ordered in 1935, these railcars were delivered in 1937 to the Central Argentine Railway. They were powered by Armstrong-Sulzer engines and seated 75.

General arrangement drawings of the Central Argentine Railways 75 seat railcars which were delivered in 1937.

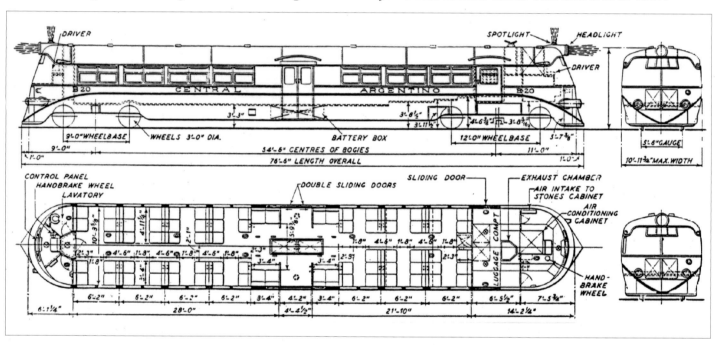

On the railway front, activity continued with a couple of notable orders being for 300 12 ton open wagons for the LMS and four single 275hp diesel railcars and a pair of articulated railcars for the Central Argentine Railway. The single units were powered by an Armstrong-Sulzer engine rated at 275hp @ 1150rpm and fitted within a power bogie which could achieve a top speed of just under 70mph. Within their length of 76ft 6ins, seating for 75 passengers, a toilet and a luggage compartment were accommodated.

These were followed in 1936 by orders for a diverse selection of products for home and overseas customers, with actual construction in most cases being completed during 1937 and early 1938. Home orders comprised 200 container flat wagons, 19 brake 3rd and 36, 3rd class coaches as part of a large shared order for the LNER and 19 3rd class electric driving trailer coaches together with 11 composite coaches for the Wirral lines of the LMS. Construction of these three-car electric multiple units for the Wirral Lines was shared with Metro-Cammell and were completed in 1938. Each of the nineteen sets included one of the BRC&W driving trailer vehicles (29271-29289) whereas the trailer composites (29702-29712) were placed within eleven of the sets. The remaining vehicles were produced by Metro-Cammell. These electric multiple units later became British Railways class 503. The LMS also placed an order for 150 20 ton coal wagons as part of a much larger requirement shared between several suppliers. Overseas, South African Railways called for 300 high-sided bogie wagons together with 13 coaches which were part of a larger order shared, once again, with Metro-Cammell. The Sao Paulo Railway of Brazil also placed an order for ten 2nd class coaches.

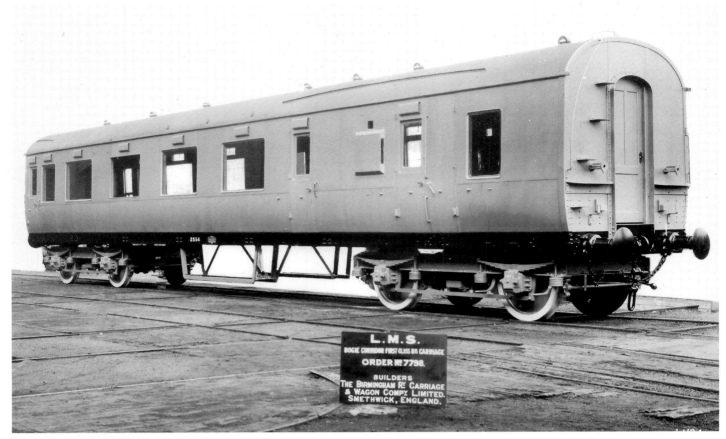

The underframes and bodywork on this LMS first class brake coach were fabricated by BRC&W. Bogies, fitting out and painting, however, were carried out at Wolverton.

A very modern looking coach for its time was this 1934 vestibule 3rd class coach awaiting delivery to the LMS.

1936 LMS vestibuled 3rd class coach No.9355 was rolled out into the sunshine to be photographed. A London trolleybus can be seen under construction in the background.

London Transport meantime was still busy building-up its trolleybus fleet and required a further 100 bodies for a batch of AEC 664T chassis. These were 70 seaters with numbers 955-1029 comprising their J2 class and 1030-1054, the J3 class. These came off the production line between February and October 1938. These, in common with most of the trolleybus fleet, were 30ft long and 7ft 6ins wide.

New Underground surface stock supply was shared between BRC&W and the Gloucester Railway Carriage and Wagon Company. This comprised the O and P series of motor cars and trailers which were introduced from 1937. BRC&W's input consisted of 114 vehicles which are detailed below.

Class	Type	Numbers	
O	Motor Car	13000-13028	14000-14028
P	Motor Car	13246-13257	14246-14257
P	Trailer Car	013258-013261	014258-014261
P	Motor Car	13262-13269	14262-14269
P	Trailer Car	013270-013273	014270-014273

Seating for 44 was provided in the trailers and 40 in the motor cars. They were 51ft 1in long, 9ft 8ins wide and 11ft 10ins high.

During the summer of 1937, Metro-Cammell received an order to build a dozen luxury air conditioned coaches for the South African Railway which were to operate as their famous 'Blue Train'. However, shortly afterwards the order was increased by a further seven vehicles and BRC&W were sub-contracted to produce these. They comprised lounge cars, dining cars, a kitchen car and baggage van with delivery taking place before the outbreak of war. The 'Blue Train' was world famous for its service and luxury and was often dubbed 'a hotel on wheels'.

London Transport orders in-build and received during 1938 kept the works busy. 1938 tube stock requirements which were completed before the war intervened comprised 271 trailer vehicles and 99 non-driving motor cars which consisted of vehicles with traction motors and control equipment but no driving positions. Trailer cars were numbered 012158-012388, 092389-092408, 012412-012421 and 012467-012476. The non-driving motor cars were 12059-12157.

The final trolleybus order was placed in May 1938 and deliveries started just before the outbreak of war in June 1939, thereafter continuing until June the following year. These 90 vehicles were again 70 seaters on AEC 664T chassis which made up the N1 class. They were numbered 1555-1644. The recently re-named Birmingham City Transport had also placed an order for a further 50 bus bodies which were numbered 151-200 and delivered the same year. The final double deck bus bodies for Birmingham were produced in 1939. These thirty vehicles were numbered 1240 to 1269 and brought the total purchased by this operator to a commendable 245. These, together with the balance of the London trolleybus orders were the last buses to be built by BRC&W; production of these vehicles not being

One of the driving trailer cars built for the Wirral Lines of the LMS in 1938. Each of the 19 3-car electric multiple units included one of these vehicles in the set.

Side view 0f 29281 built in 1938 for the LMS Wirral Lines. This 3rd class coach was a driving trailer car.

resumed again after the war. And so the company reverted back to being an exclusive rolling stock builder – but not for long – as the war saw the factory, once again, producing endless streams of armaments and implements of war. The LNER placed orders in 1938 for the supply of 250 10 ton covered wagons and for 100 driving trailer coaches.

July produced the first of many orders from the War Office, the initial requirement being for 175 A10 heavy cruiser tanks. These were constructed by a number of manufacturers with BRC&W taking the bulk. They were completed by September 1940 and were built by Vickers (10), Metro-Cammell (45), and BRC&W (120). They were used in France and North Africa but by late 1941 they were obsolete and replaced by improved machines. They weighed in at 14 tons and had a crew of 5. The 6 cylinder AEC petrol engines fitted were rated at 150 bhp and could achieve 16 mph. Armament comprised a 2pdr gun and 2 machine guns. War Office orders continued to arrive during 1939 for tens of thousands of shell forgings and for Valentine infantry tanks which were completed in 1941.

Turkish State Railways ordered 114 pairs of twin 4-wheeled hopper wagons but owing to the outbreak of war only 12 pairs were actually completed. French Railways were disappointed too. They wanted 2000 long wheelbase covered wagons but only 175 had been built before France was over-run. An order which was completed, however, was for the British Iron and Steel Corporation who required 150 hopper ore wagons.

Notes from the reports of the Company's Annual General Meetings give a view of BRC&W's fortunes as seen from the board room. Wages paid to continental workers were considerably lower (estimated to be between 45% and 70% lower) than those paid in Britain which put the company at a disadvantage when trying to obtain orders. Prices were necessarily higher than those quoted by competitors across the Channel. Another factor identified as affecting orders was the practice of railway companies building their own rolling stock.

From the late 1920s into the 1930s, the Company's workshops were under-employed resulting in decreased profits and trading losses before a slow upturn in fortunes emerged during the latter part of the decade. The reported profit for 1929 was just under £94,000 whereas by 1932 the depression had intensified to a point where the profit was down to just under £61,000 which prompted salary cuts and lay-offs together with cuts in directors fees. The following year, profit was down again to just over £22,000 and in 1934 a loss approaching £13,000 was reported. Export orders which had accounted for some 50%-75% of the Company's workload had slumped dramatically with demand having reached an all time low.

Regarding the French works owned by BRC&W, this was sold in 1932, but the company's organisation in France had been successful in securing some useful orders.

But from the mid 1930s a steady improvement was under way at Smethwick with profits once again appearing on the balance sheet. Those for 1935 amounted to £3,300 with 1936 yielding just under £52,000. This was further improved the following year with a profit of £56,500.

N1 class trolleybus No.1642 was part of the final order for these vehicles. Deliveries of these 70 seat AEC 664Ts continued until the middle of 1940.
PHOTO: J.C.GILLHAM

Twin hopper wagons supplied to the Turkish State Railway, an order interrupted by the outbreak of war.

CHAPTER 4

At War Again

The second world war saw the company change direction again in its building programme, with the production of armaments taking priority and almost exclusively filling the order book. This necessarily saw the plant and its production layout undergo radical changes to meet the new demands placed upon it.

Two key areas of production at Smethwick concentrated on heavy armoured fighting vehicles and gliders. In addition, main components such as fuselages and wings for Blenheim, Halifax and Lancaster bombers were produced as well as hundreds of thousands of shells, bombs and to a lesser extent, depth charges. Over 400 scout car bodies for Daimler were also built. Among other contemporary builders, BRC&W was one of the most prolific tank manufacturers and produced large quantities of Valentines, Churchills and Cromwells. The company, in co-operation with the Ministry of Supply also carried out a great deal of experimental design and development work on both these and a number of other heavy armoured vehicles. Indeed, BRC&W were responsible for producing the prototypes of several other fighting vehicles.

One of the company's foremen, Joe 'Joby' Butler played an important part in the war effort through an observation he had made. He had been watching a machine which was able to move in a circle through the use of ball-bearings and it occurred to him that a tank's gun turret could swivel much more easily by adopting the same principle. After sending details to the Government, his idea was put into practice and 'Joby' was awarded an OBE for his inventiveness.

BRC&W constructed a tank transporter train for their delivery and the testing of completed tanks was carried out on a nearby piece of farmland.

The Valentine Mk III was the first wartime tank to be built by the company, with over 900 coming off the production line from 1941. Designed as an infantry co-operation tank with a crew of 4, a 2 pdr gun and a machine gun, it was more generally deployed as a cruiser, being widely used in North Africa. Weighing-in at 17 tons, the Valentine was powered by an AEC A189 131hp diesel engine and could travel at 15mph. Its chassis was also used as the basis of a scissors bridgelayer, with 160 at least being built by BRC&W from 1942. Additionally, the chassis were also used for

A10 Cruiser tanks under construction at Smethwick during 1940.

55

Tank hulls, possibly A10s, under construction during World War 2.

A10 Cruiser being put through its paces before being handed over in 1940.

Completed A10 Cruiser awaits its first tour of duty as it prepares to leave the BRC&W factory in 1940.

the Archer 17 pdr tank destroyer and the Bishop 25 pdr self propelled gun of which it is thought the company built 150.

Next came the A22 Churchill which was a tank designed to assist the infantry cross heavily shelled ground and attack strongly defended positions. Deliveries commenced in 1941 and the Churchill, equipped with a 2 pdr gun and two machine guns, was first used in the Dieppe raids of August 1942 before being deployed in North Africa, mainly in Tunisia. The tank's final theatre of operation was in the North West Europe campaign. Its weight, at 38 tons, was more than twice that of the Valentine as was its powerpack, which comprised Bedford twin-six petrol engines producing 350bhp which acheived 8mph across country. A crew of 5 was carried. Along with the Valentines, a number of Churchills also saw service with the Russian Army.

During 1940, a General Staff Specification was produced for a heavy duty cruiser tank. One of these became the A27 Cromwell and BRC&W took on the design work for the final version of the Cromwell which emerged in prototype form in January 1942. This was put through its paces so that any teething problems could be ironed-out before going onto the battlefield. As a result they didn't go into mass production until January 1943, but the testing produced what became a fast and reliable tank which saw service in Normandy and Belgium. Like the Churchill, they carried a crew of 5 but with their powerful 600hp Rolls Royce Meteor engines, the Cromwells could carry their weight of 27.5 tons at 18mph across country. Their main armament

consisted of a 6 pdr gun and a couple of machine guns.

The company also designed and produced the A30 Challenger cruiser tank which entered production at the end of 1943 with some 200 being assembled the following year. A 17 pdr gun was featured together with a machine gun. They too, also incorporated the Rolls Royce Meteor 600hp V12 petrol engine which moved these 32.5 ton tanks across country at 25mph. Some of these machines saw service in Holland.

Last to be produced was the Leyland designed Avenger tank destroyer equipped with a 17 pdr anti-tank gun and a machine gun. These were not completed, however, until after hostilities had ceased. Power for these 31 ton machines was derived once again by the Rolls Royce Meteor petrol engine producing a top speed of 32mph.

Aircraft component production commenced in the carriage workshops in 1938. These fabrications were no strangers to Smethwick as aircraft had been built and flown from there during the previous conflict. Indeed, some of the very first multi-engined heavy bombers ever built had been produced by the company at that time. The giant all-wood Hamilcar heavy transport glider was the main type of complete aircraft built by BRC&W during the second world war and was the largest glider available to the allies. These had a cavernous hold sufficient to carry a tank or other heavy loads including Bren gun carriers, Jeeps, and Daimler scout cars. Indeed, a payload of 64 men and a couple of Jeeps was adequately accommodated. BRC&W had the distinction of building not only the tanks but also

Churchill tanks were produced by BRC&W from 1941.

BRC&W started building these Cromwell tanks in large numbers from the beginning of 1943.

A Challenger tank is pictured in BRC&W's frame shop in 1944. It still needs some external fitting out to be done before it is ready to leave.

Challenger tanks started coming off the production line during 1944.

The Avenger was the final type of tank to be built by BRC&W. They were completed after hostilities had ceased.

the aircraft that transported them to battle. March 1942 marked the maiden flight of the prototype Hamilcar before its designers, the General Aircraft Co., placed orders for its wholesale production. BRC&W was the main building contractor, producing a significant number of the 412 gliders which were completed. Crewed by a pilot and co-pilot, they took part in the successful D Day operation as well as in subsequent airborne operations at Wesel and Arnhem. The main dimensions of these giant Hamilcars are shown below:-

Wing span	110ft
Fuselage length	68ft 6ins
Fuselage height	20ft 4ins
Weight with cargo	36,000lbs
Maximum towing speed	150mph
Tow planes	Halifax, Lancaster, Stirling

Towards the end of hostilities, BRC&W produced a plane called the Albarmar which was constructed entirely of magnesium and incorporated built-in radar. Only two were made and no further details or pictures are known to exist.

Great demands were placed upon the company on several occasions to increase the production of both tanks and aircraft, all of which they were able to meet, in addition to producing radar units as well. Despite most of the company's resources being dedicated almost exclusively to war work, they were, nevertheless, able to stretch production even further towards the end of the war and make a start on producing much needed wagons for both the home and overseas markets. Previous rolling stock requirements for the Ministry of Supply had been met during the early stages of the war and included some 500 20 ton hopper wagons, 200 open goods wagons and 60 refrigerated wagons.

At BRC&W's Annual General Meeting in 1945, the company reported a profit of £85,000 for the previous year. Sir Bernard Docker KBE, JP, Chairman, included in his statement:

I am sure you (the shareholders) will appreciate the co-operation which has taken place between the management and the employees, so largely due to the extraordinary able leadership of Mr Moyses and which has made possible the output of so much war material, and on your behalf I would express our thanks to Mr Moyses, the executives, staff and workpeople for their hard work and enthusiasm and in so doing we do not forget those in the services whose safe and speedy return we now look forward to at an early date.

In thanking the chairman and directors, Mr George Beech on behalf of the shareholders said:

The information given by the chairman was impressive and proved conclusively the important contribution made by the company towards the attainment of victory.

One of the giant Hamilcar gliders built by BRC&W in 1943.

This view of a completed Hamilcar glider inside BRC&W's factory shows its enormous proportions to advantage.

Recovery and Renewal – Overseas

With the production of war machines at an end, BRC&W returned once again to the peaceable business of building railway vehicles, after re-arranging the factory to facilitate normal production. The company celebrated its centenary in 1955 and during its 100 year history and beyond, BRC&W made a significant and important contribution to railways across the globe. Indeed, over this period they had designed and constructed countless types of railway vehicles to suit virtually every condition and climate imaginable. By 1950, the works covered an area of over 50 acres and provided employment for around 3000 workers. The North Works carried out coach building, painting, upholstering and fitting out of rolling stock while the South Works specialised in steel construction, metal fabrication and welding. Between them they carried out everything required to produce the variety and quality of rolling stock that the company was renowned for.

Following the war, in addition to producing carriages and wagons for both home and overseas customers, BRC&W established itself in the diesel traction field by producing both diesel-electric locomotives and railcars. Locomotives of various designs were built for the Commonwealth Railways of Australia, Sierra Leone, Eire and Ghana and were quite different in appearance to those constructed for British Railways.

Smethwick produced a quantity of diesel railcars for overseas railways which included New Zealand, Nyasaland and Nigeria together with an order for articulated units for Egypt. The company also built electric multiple units for South Africa and Sao Paulo.

Many overseas railways ordered coaching stock and freight vehicles after the war, with the former being required by customers spread among such countries as Argentina, Antofagasta, Iraq, Malaya, India and Nigeria.

Freight Wagons

Many thousands of wagons of virtually every description and type were supplied to overseas railways by BRC&W and a selection of these are illustrated. Customers included railway operators in Australia, Argentina, Burma, Brazil, Buenos Aires, Columbia, Egypt, East Africa, Hong Kong, India, Iraq, Malaya, Nigeria, New Zealand, Palestine, Peru, Rhodesia, Sudan, South Africa and Turkey.

20 ton covered goods wagon built after the war for the Ministry of Supply. Built as part of the post-war United Nations plan for rehabilitation of railways, it almost certainly would have gone to Eastern Europe.

30 ton bogie lowsided wagon (braked) seen before departure to the Egyptian State Railway in 1947.

1947 30 ton unbraked bogie box wagon for the Egyptian State Railway.

1948 unbraked 10 ton open lowsided wagon for the Egyptian State Railway.

15 ton covered goods wagon built for Sudan Railways after the war.

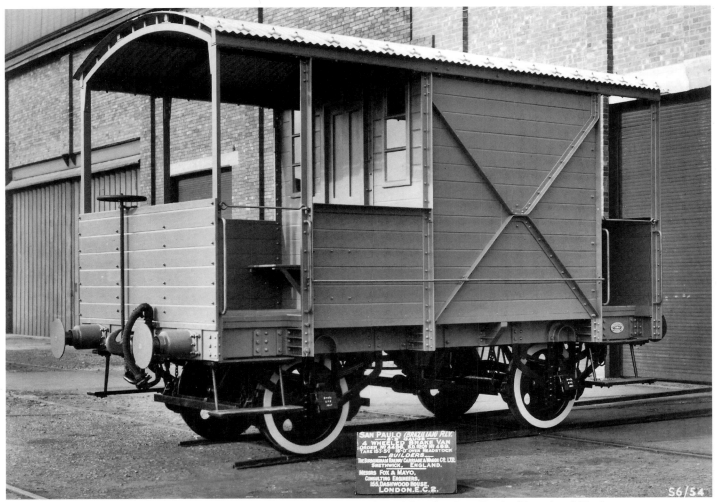

This neat 4-wheel brake van dates back to 1948 and was produced for the San Paulo (Brazilian) Railway.

56 ton bogie brake van destined for the 5ft 6in. gauge San Martin railway in the Republic of Argentina during the early 50s.

Hong Kong was the destination for this 1952 bogie goods brake van.

1952 45 ton bogie highsided wagon for the Hong Kong Railway.

1951 sheep wagon for the New Zealand Railways. The wagon will receive its wooden sides on arrival in New Zealand.

1960 bogie goods brake van for the Nigerian Railway Corporation.

Eleven of these streamlined 3-car articulated units were delivered to the Egyptian State Railways in 1951. These 400hp units were used on suburban and branch line duties.

Articulated railcars were very much in vogue with overseas railways and New Zealand Railways took delivery of the first of its order for 35 air braked, articulated twin-car diesel-mechanical units numbered RM100-RM134, in January 1955. These 88 seat units were built in association with the Drewry Car Company and were powered by two Fiat engines through Vulcan-Sinclair fluid couplings and Wilson-Drewry five speed epicyclic gearboxes. Accommodation for 36 passengers was provided in the first coach with reversible reclining seats, and for 52 passengers in the second coach. Up to three of these units could be worked together in multiple.

Additional Information
    Length over headstocks –105ft
    Overall width – 8ft 10ins
    Overall height – 11 ft3ins
    Weight in working order – 57.15 tons
    Maximum speed – 65mph
    Engines (two) – Fiat 6 cyl type 700.040
    B.H.P. (each) – 210
    Wheel diameter – 2ft 7ins

BRC&W was again associated with the Drewry Car Company in building two single diesel-mechanical railcars for use on the 3ft 6in gauge Nyasaland Railways system. Entering service c.1957, they were powered by a Fiat engine which drove the inner axle of one bogie through a Vulcan-Sinclair fluid coupling and a Wilson-Drewry four speed epicyclic gearbox. Accommodation for 15 first class and 12 second class passengers was specified along with two toilets and a kitchenette. Although there was a driving compartment at each end of the car, the full width cab at one end was not matched by the other! It consisted merely of a small cubicle for emergency use only, rather than for normal driving purposes.

Additional Information
    Weight in working order – 33 tons
    Engine – Fiat 6 cyl type 700
    B.H.P. – 210
    Maximum speed – 51mph
    Length over headstocks – 59ft 1ins

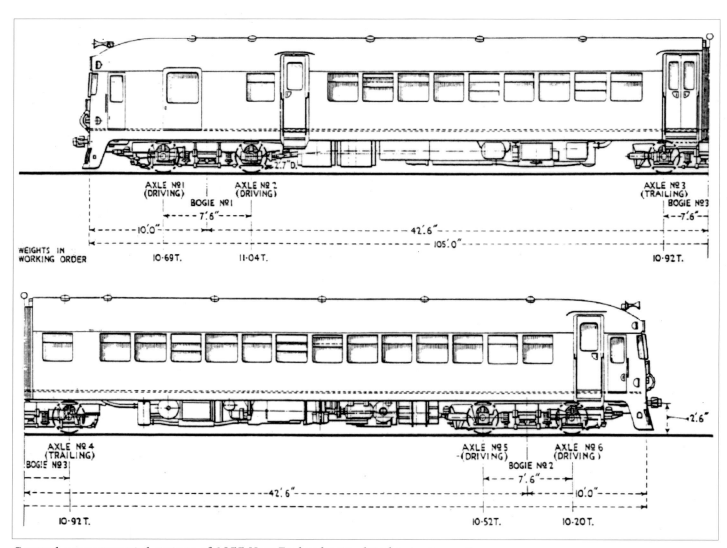

General arrangement drawings of 1955 New Zealand articulated twin-car units.

Above: New Zealand Railways ordered 35 of these articulated twin-car diesel-mechanical units. These started arriving in New Zealand in January 1955.

Right: This photograph shows the driving cab of one of the New Zealand articulated twin-car units of 1955.

Two of these diesel-mechanical railcars were built for service in Nyasaland.

Plan showing the internal layout of the Nyasaland railcars.

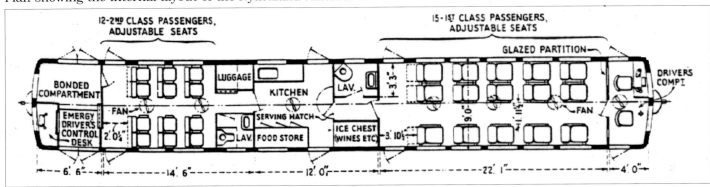

Plan showing the layout of the power car of the Nigerian twin-car sets.

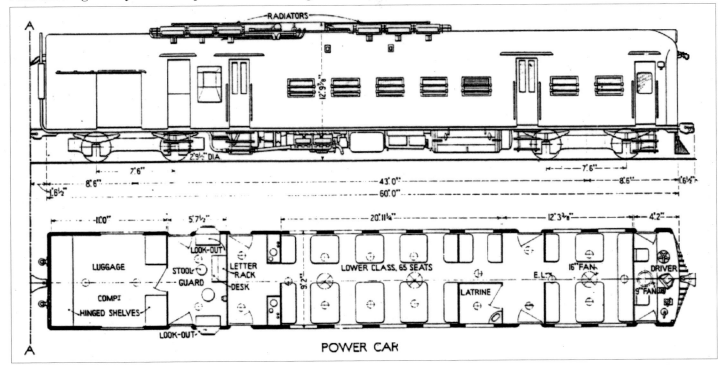

POWER CAR

The last of the overseas railcars went to the Nigerian Railway Corporation for their 3ft 6in network. Once again, the BRC&W and Drewry association combined to build two, twin-unit, vacuum braked, diesel railcars which were completed in the late fifties. Each set comprised one power car and one control trailer and provided seating for 139 third class and nine second class passengers. Internal arrangement of the cars was as follows :-

Power Car – 65 third class seats, toilet, guards and luggage compartments.
Control trailer – 9 second class seats, 74 third class seats, 2 toilets.

Third class seating consisted of covered seat squabs with wooden slatted back rests. Fully automatic Wilson epicyclic gearboxes were featured which were controlled by Self Changing Gears VS automatic control, and up to four of these units could be worked together in multiple. Two banks of external roof mounted radiators (one bank per engine) provided engine cooling.

Additional Information
Total weight – 60.25 tons
Length per car – 60 ft 0ins
Engines (two) – B.U.T/Leyland 6 cylinder
B.H.P. (each) – 200 @ 1900rpm
Width over bodysides – 9ft 2ins
Height to roof sheets – 12 ft 2ins
Maximum speed – 50mph
Wheel diameter – 2 ft 9.5ins

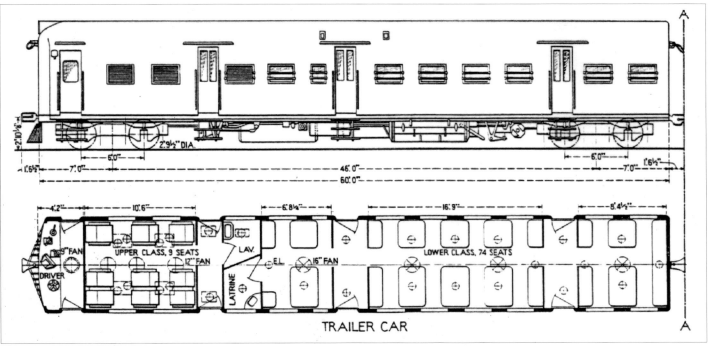

Plan showing the layout of the trailer car of the Nigerian twin-car sets.

Two pairs of these twin-car diesel-mechanical railcars were built in the late 1950s for the Nigerian Railway Corporation. Note the roof-mounted radiators.

Electric Multiple Units

Three 3-car electric multiple units were designed and built in collaboration with main contractor English Electric for the Santos Jundiai Brazil Railway. They were ordered to provide a fast service between Sao Paulo and its suburbs with each unit providing a total seating capacity of 198. Air operated sliding doors were included and traction motors and all electrical equipment was produced by English Electric. Overhead lines provided the 3000 volt power supply for these 800hp units and all cars were fitted with Westinghouse electro-pneumatic brakes.

Metro Cammell subcontracted the building of a quantity of electric multiple units to BRC&W for the 3ft 6in Reef system of South African Railways. These comprised 35 third class motor coaches and 88 1st class trailers together with 33 third class trailers, all of which were constructed with sliding doors. They ran from a 3000 volt DC overhead supply and were formed as 8 car sets comprising six trailers with a motor car at each end. Body length per car was 60 ft 3ins and the width over body was 9 ft 3ins.

Several orders totalling at least 43 vacuum braked motor coaches for service in South Africa were also placed with the company. Some of these were for the Cape Western system and featured MetroVick electrical equipment which was energised by two collapsible pantographs on the coach roof.

Additional Information

Body length over head stocks – 60ft 6ins
Width over body panels – 9 ft 1ins
Height over lowered pantographs – 13ft 7ins
Seating capacity – 69

The early fifties also saw electric trailer cars being supplied to India in the shape of 24 for the Bombay, Baroda and Central India Railway and 32 for the Great India Peninsular Railway.

Three-car electric multiple unit built for the Santos A Jundiai Railway of Brazil.

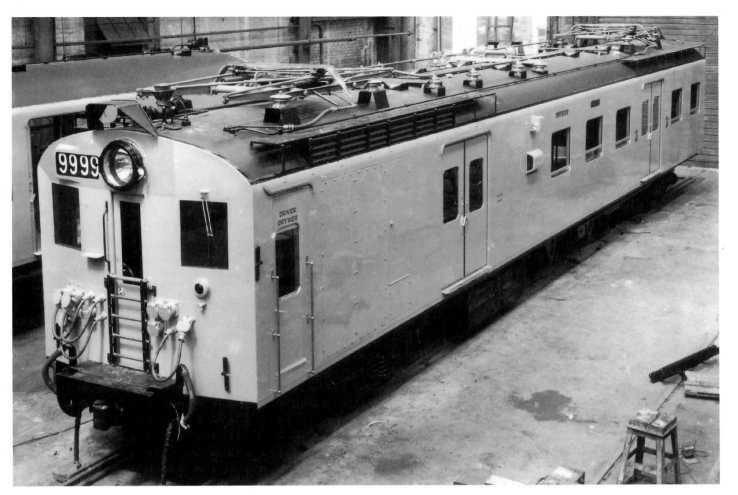

Above: This 3rd class baggage and motor car was built in 1952 for South African Railways. 35 of these electric cars were constructed.

Right: This photograph shows the driving cab of one of the South African 3rd class baggage and motor cars.

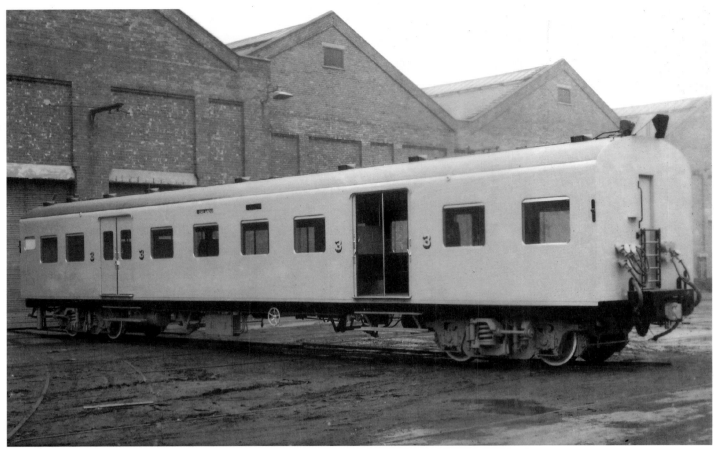

Thirty three of these 3rd class trailers were delivered to South African Railways from 1952.

The Bombay Baroda and Central India Railway ordered 24 of these trailer cars for use within electric multiple units.

Coaches

A quantity of standard gauge passenger coaches together with luggage and brake vans were completed during 1950 for Iraq. These comprised 121-seater third class coaches, luggage and brake vans, 1st/2nd class sleeper composite coaches with and without air conditioning, and some air conditioned 1st/2nd class sleeper composite coaches incorporating a kitchen.

Additional Information
Length over end panels – 73ft 7ins
Width over body panels – 9ft 9ins
Height to roof sheets – 13ft 3ins

Malayan State Railways also received coaching stock for their metre gauge system with the supply of the following types of vehicles concluding in 1951:-

Third class coaches, 2nd/3rd class composite coaches, pressure ventilated 1st class night cars, pressure ventilated 1st/2nd class night cars, air conditioned first class day and night cars and air conditioned 1st class buffet cars.

Additional Information
Length over end panels – 60ft 11ins
Width over bodyside panels – 8ft 11ins
Height to roof sheets – 12ft 0ins

An advertisement proclaiming **Pullman Coaches for South America** shows one of the three special first class coaches which were built and shipped to the Antofagasta (Chile) and Bolivia Railway in 1955.

During the mid 1950s Nigerian Railways received 80 all-steel passenger vehicles from BRC&W which were made up as follows:-

50 3rd class coaches, 6 third class brake coaches, 6 3rd class canteen coaches, 9 1st/2nd class day cars, 2 second class sleepers, 3 1st/2nd class sleepers, 3 1st class sleepers and an ivory coloured luxury 52ft long saloon coach for use by the Governor and for special occasions. The special saloon was designed for use as a mobile hotel and included an air conditioned, fully furnished and fitted lounge and bedroom, separate bathroom and toilet and an engine generator room to supply power for lighting and air conditioning. A further order for an additional 72 passenger coaches of various specifications was also built by the company for Nigeria.

Passenger coaches were also constructed for Argentina, the Iraq Petroleum Company, India and South Africa.

1950 luggage and brake van built for Iraqi State Railways.

1950 air conditioned 1st/2nd class coach with kitchen for Iraqi State Railways.

1951 third class coach for Malayan Railways.

Interior view of 1951 third class coach for Malayan Railways.

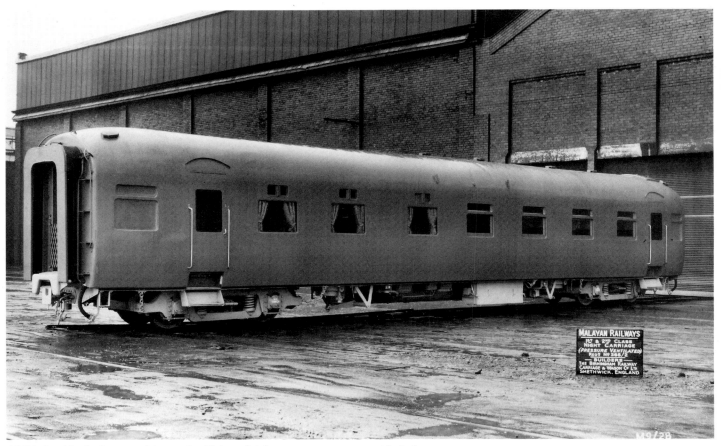

1951 1st/2nd class night coach. This vehicle was pressure ventilated.

Nigerian Railways took delivery of scores of coaches and wagons during the 1950s. This 3rd class brake car was built towards the end of the decade.

1955 1st/2nd class sleeping car produced for the Nigerian Railway Corporation.

Third class canteen car for Nigerian Railways.

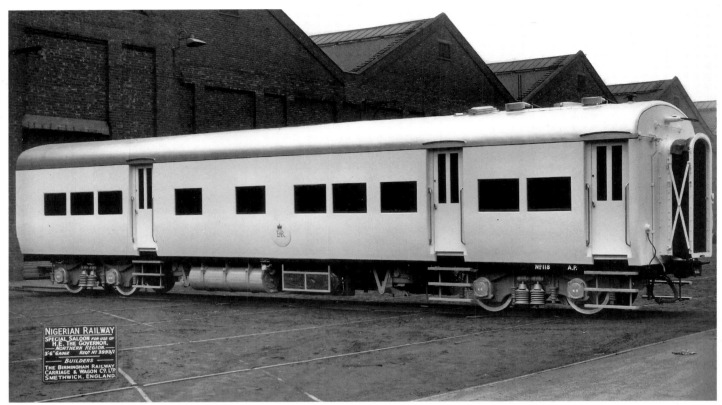

This special saloon was built in 1955 for the Nigerian Railway for the use of the Governor and was finished in an ivory livery. Fitted out like a mobile hotel, this car was also air-conditioned.

This view shows the lounge in the special saloon kept by Nigerian Railways for the use of the Governor.

During the 1950s BRC&W constructed coaches for the Iraqi Petroleum Company. Pictured is a 3rd class brake coach which was fitted out with wooden seats.

The inside of one of the Iraqi Petroleum Company's 3rd class brake coaches showing the spartan nature of the interior and the wooden seats.

1947 1st/3rd class composite coach built for the Southern Railway and delivered to British Railways.

1948 first class corridor coach ordered by the LNER and delivered to British Railways.

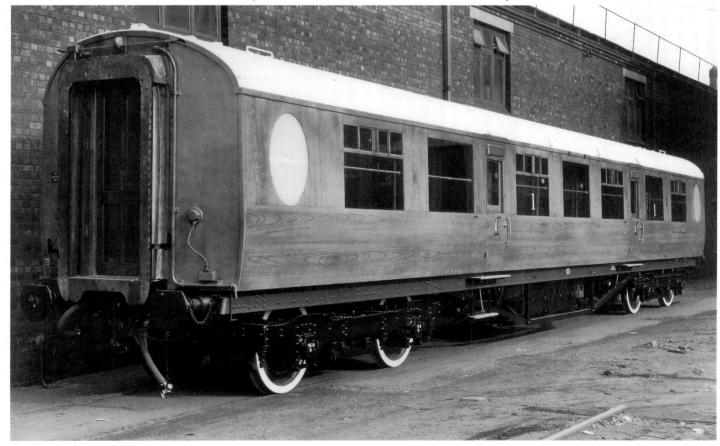

Recovery and Renewal – Britain

The ravages of war had wreaked havoc with our railways and recovery and renewal was urgently needed to get the system back into full swing again. As far as rolling stock was concerned, BRC&W helped in the process by filling orders for both passenger and freight vehicles for the 'Big Four' and then for the newly created British Railways. Indeed, since the war over 19,000 freight vehicles of many different kinds were supplied and just under 1000 coaches, excluding diesel and electric multiple units. Modernisation was the order of the day and the British Railways Modernisation Plan kept the factory busy for several years up to the point of closure.

Top: 1951 4-wheel wagon for use within the factory confines of Steel Peech and Tozer.
Bottom: United Steel Corporation 75 ton bogie bloom wagon which was for internal factory use. This was built in 1962.

1954 30 ton bogie bolster for British Railways.

1956 21 ton hopper produced for British Railways

1958 16 ton mineral wagon for British Railways.

1958 20 ton ballast brake van showing its plough in the lowered position.

Brake/3rd class coach ordered by the Southern Railway and completed in 1948. This too, was delivered into British Railways ownership.

Over 600 Mk1 coaches were produced to a variety of specifications between 1953 and 1961 and the table below details these in sequence of orders.

Into Service	BR Numbers	Type
1953/54	24332-24396	Corridor 3rd
1954	3003-3019	Open 1st
1953/54	24576-24675	Corridor 3rd
1955	15585-15596	Composite 1st/3rd
1955	15597-15624	Composite 1st/3rd
1954/55	24796-24818	Corridor 3rd
1955/56	80725-80802	Brake Vans
1956	4258-4357	Open 3rd
1956/57	4413-4472	Open 3rd
1957	4473-4487	Open 3rd
1957	3081	Open 1st Prototype first class open saloon with re-designed interior and double glazing
1957	4637	Open 2nd Prototype 2nd class open saloon
1959	4810-4829	Open 2nd
1959	3085-3094	Open 1st
1959/60	1925-1943	Restaurant Unclassified
1960/61	1701-1738	Restaurant Buffet
1961	306-309	Restaurant 1st
1959	3095-3100	Open 1st
1961	1739-1754	Restaurant Buffet

Mk1 open first coach built in 1959 and initially used by the Western Region.

Electric Multiple Units

Electrification of the Liverpool Street-Shenfield line took place in September 1949 and required the use of ninety two 3-car electric multiple units. The construction of these was shared between BRC&W and Metro-Cammell, with the latter building both the driving motor cars and trailers for each set. BRC&W constructed the 60-seat driving trailers which were numbered 65601-65692. These units worked from an overhead 1500V DC supply and featured air operated sliding doors and electro-pneumatic brakes. Overall length was 55ft 4ins and the overall width, 9ft 3ins

1954 saw delivery of 1500 volt DC electric multiple units (later class 506) for the Manchester-Glossop/Hadfield service. These comprised eight 3-car sets which were constructed jointly between BRC&W and Metro-Cammell. BRC&W's contribution was the driving trailer second vehicle in each set which were allotted numbers 59601-59608.

These were followed in 1956 by further 3-car electric multiple units, this time for the Wirral Lines. These worked on 650 volts DC and again were constructed jointly by BRC&W and Metro-Cammell. 24 sets (later class 503) were delivered, each of which included a BRC&W driving trailer second vehicle which were numbered 29131-29154. Ten of the units also included a BRC&W trailer composite within their formations which were numbered 29821-29830. Electro-pneumatic sliding doors and air brakes were featured on these units. A couple of extra vehicles of each type were also built as replacements for cars in the 1938 sets and these were numbered 29155/56 and 29831/32.

	Driving Trailer	Trailer Composite
Length over end panels	58ft 0in	56ft 0in
Width over side panels	8ft 8in	8ft 8in
Height to roof sheets	11ft 5in	11ft 5in

What were later to become class 104 diesel multiple units entered service during 1957/58. They were used on both the Eastern and London Midland Regions in 2, 3 and 4-car formations. One of the Eastern Region's 4-car units is pictured.

Diesel Multiple Units

A total of 302 vacuum braked, diesel-mechanical multiple cars (later class 104) were built in collaboration with Drewry as part of the 1955 Modernisation Plan, which were formed into 2, 3, or 4 car units. These came on stream during 1957/58 and were split between the Eastern and London Midland Regions.

Each motor car was fitted with two underfloor B.U.T (Leyland) 6 cylinder 150bhp engines. Transmission was provided by means of a Wilson 4-speed epicyclic gearbox and fluid coupling, which reached the inner axle of the adjacent bogie by means of a cardan shaft and spur and bevel final drive. Heating was provided by means of Smith-Webasto oil burners which used the same fuel oil as the engines. The various car types and numbers together with their formations and initial region of delivery are shown:

Driving Motor Brake Second – 52 second class seats
    50420-50423 (LMR 3-car)
    50428-50479 (LMR 3-car)
    50532-50541 (LMR 2-car)
    50594-50598 (ER 2-car)

Driving Motor Composite – 12 first class seats and 51 second class (LMR 54 seats)
    50424-50427 (LMR 3-car)
    50480-50531 (LMR 3-car)
    50542-50593 (ER 4-car)

Driving Trailer Composite – 12 first class seats and 54 second class
    56175-56184 (LMR 2-car)
    56185-56189 (ER 2-car)

Trailer Composite – 12 first class seats and 54 second class
    59132-59187 (LMR 3-car)

Trailer Brake Second – 51 second class seats
    59209-59229 (ER 4-car)
    59240-59244 (ER 4-car)

Trailer Second – 69 second class seats
    59188-59208 (ER 4-car)
    59230-59234 (ER 4-car)

Additional Information
    Weight of motor cars – 31 tons
    Weight of trailer cars – 24 or 25 tons
    Overall Width – 9ft 3in
    Length of driving cars – 57ft 6ins
    Length of non-driving cars – 57ft 0in
    Maximum speed – 70mph

Further diesel multiple units were built, which were later to become class 118, and were introduced on the Western Region in 1960. Their motor cars were also powered by pairs of underfloor B.U.T (Leyland) 6 cylinder 150bhp engines. This class comprised fifteen 3-car units, the details of which follow:-

Driving Motor Brake Second – 65 Second class seats
    51302-51316

Driving Motor Second – 91 Second class seats
    51317-51331

Trailer Composite – 22 First class seats and 48 second class
    59469-59483

Additional Information
    Weight of motor cars – 36 tons
    Weight of trailer cars – 30 tons
    Overall width – 9ft 3ins
    Length of driving cars – 64ft
    Length of non-driving cars – 63ft 10ins
    Maximum speed – 70mph

Introduced in 1961, the final class of units comprising 90 cars was destined for the Eastern Region and later became class 110. These ran as thirty 3-car units, with motor cars being powered by pairs of underfloor 180bhp Rolls Royce engines:-

Driving Motor Brake Composite – 12 First class seats and 33 second class
    51809-51828
    52066-52075

Driving Motor Composite – 12 First class seats and 54 second class
    51829-51848
    52076-52085

Trailer Second – 72 Second class seats
    59693-59712
    59808-59817

Additional Information
    Weight of motor cars – 32 tons (DMBC), 31.5 tons (DMC)
    Weight of trailer cars – 24 tons
    Overall width – 9ft 3ins
    Length of all cars – 57ft 6ins
    Maximum speed – 70mph

1960 saw the introduction of these 3-car units which were later to become class 118 sets. These were all allocated to the Western Region.

These 3-car diesel multiple units, (later class 110), were put to use by the Eastern Region from 1961.

Locomotives

BRC&W were responsible for building 239 locomotives for British Railways embracing four different classes. These ranged from Type 2 and Type 3 diesel-electric machines to a class of 100mph, Type AL1 main line electric locomotives.

The first to emerge were 47 Type 2 Bo-Bo diesel-electric locos, numbered D5300-D5346, which were delivered to the Eastern and Scottish Regions during 1958 and 1959 and later became class 26. Connecting doors were featured at the end of each cab to facilitate access between locos when working in multiple. When in passenger use, steam heating was provided by means of a Stone-Vapor oil fired boiler. Fibreglass was used for both the inner and outer skins of the cab roofs as well as for the translucent detachable roof cover over the engine.

These locomotives had straight air brakes, but for working with fitted stock, control of the air brakes was through a triple valve operated by the train vacuum brake control. Power was derived from a Sulzer 6LDA28A engine coupled directly to a Crompton Parkinson CG391A1 main generator. This was a single-bearing 10 pole machine with separately excited, self excited, decompounding and starting windings continuously rated at 757kW, 1720 amps, 440 volts @ 750rpm. The auxiliary generator was an 8 pole machine rated at 57kW and 110 volts. The four Crompton-Parkinson traction motors, connected in parallel across the main generator, were axle-hung, nose suspended, series-wound and force ventilated machines with a continuous rating of 224hp, 430 amps and 440 volts.

Additional Information

BRC&W Works numbers – DEL 45-91
Engine – Sulzer 6LDA28-A
B.H.P – 1160 @ 750rpm
Electrical equipment – Crompton Parkinson
Control Equipment – Allen West
Weight in working order – 77.5 tons (D5300-19),
   74 tons (others)
Wheel diameter – 3ft 7ins
Overall length – 50ft 9ins
Height – 12ft 8ins
Overall width – 9ft 3ins
Top speed – 75mph
Max. tractive effort – 42,000lbs

Construction of the very first purpose built AC electric locomotives for British Railways was sub-contracted to BRC&W by Associated Electrical Industries. Numbered E3001-E3023 and E3096/97, later to become class 81, these 3,300hp, 25kV, 50 cycle locomotives were allocated to the London Midland Region for use on the West Coast Main Line. Delivered between late 1959 and 1962, with E3096 following in 1963 and E3097 almost a year later, they cost £70,000 each, and were initially classified as AL1s. The 25 locos were identical in all respects other than for the last two which were lower geared than the rest for freight duties. These were designated type B whereas the other 23 were type A. Four, 6 pole AEI series wound, force ventilated traction motors which were connected permanantly in parallel, provided the pulling power and were continuously rated at 975 volts, 700 amps and

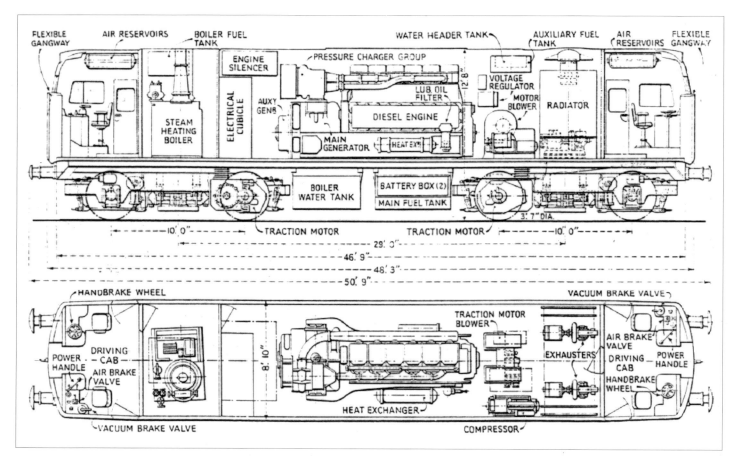

Above: General arrangement drawing of the 1160hp Type 2 (later class 26) locomotives. 47 of these were produced during 1958/59, numbered D5300-D5346.

Right: One of the AL1 (later class 81) AC electric locomotives under construction at Smethwick. 25 of these were built from 1959 and were numbered E3001-23, E3096/97.

847hp. Instead of an engine compartment as in diesel-electric locos, this space was occupied by the control gear, transformers and mercury arc rectifiers. The transformer oil was cooled by means of two pump-assisted radiators which were cooled by fans and located under the roof.

Current was collected from the overhead by one of the two Stone-Faiveley pantographs and fed through a roof mounted Brown Boveri air blast circuit breaker to the main transformer. The transformer output was converted to direct current for the traction motors by three air-cooled six-anode pumpless steel-tank mercury arc rectifiers, diametrically connected in parallel. A glass fibre fairing extended the full length of the loco between the two cabs and some of the detachable roof sections were also constructed in glass fibre. The double skin cab roof was also moulded in this material.

The braking system comprised a vacuum controlled straight air brake which operated an air pressure brake on the loco in conjunction with a vacuum brake application on the train. An independent air brake valve was fitted for use when running light or with unfitted trains. Electric train heating was also produced by these locos.

Additional Information

BRC&W works nos. – 1083-1107
Wheel arrangement – Bo-Bo
Weight – 80 tons
Wheel diameter – 4ft
Height (pantograph down) – 13ft
Length over buffers – 56ft 6ins
Width over bodysides – 8ft 8ins
Top speed – 100mph (A), 80mph (B)
Tractive effort – 48,000lbs (A), 60,000lbs (B)

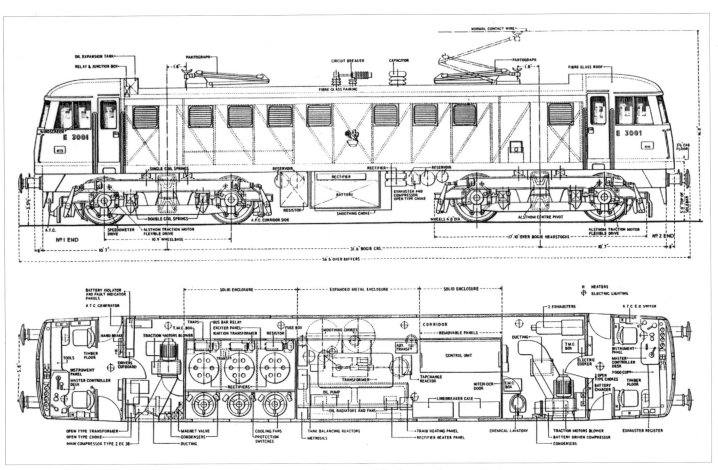

General arrangement drawing of the AL1 (later class 81) type AC electric locomotives.

The Southern Region were the recipients of the first diesel-electric locomotives to provide electric train heating exclusively. They also have the distinction of being the first and only BR locos to be powered by Sulzer 8LDA28A power units, most of which were in fact built by Vickers Armstrong at Barrow in Furness. The 98 mixed traffic 1550hp Type 3s (later to become class 33) were numbered D6500-D6597 and were delivered between 1959 and 1962. The final twelve machines were built eight inches narrower than their counterparts for use on the restricted Hastings line. In their general appearance, these Type 3s bore strong similarities with the BRC&W Type 2s but did not include front end communicating doors. Instead, they featured a two character headcode display behind the centre cab window in keeping with normal SR practice. Within each cab the driving controls are duplicated, enabling the loco to be driven from either side.

Their Crompton Parkinson C171C2 traction motors are force ventilated, series wound, axle hung and nose suspended to the bogie frame and are continuously rated at 305hp, 440 amps and 580 volts. These are connected in parallel across the main generator. The traction generator (CG391B1) is a single bearing 10 pole machine with separately excited, self excited, decompouding and starting windings continuously rated at 1012kW, 1760 amps 575 volts @ 750rpm. The Crompton Parkinson generator grouping also includes the train heat (CAG392A1) and auxiliary (CAG193A1) generators which are continuously rated at 250kW, 313 amps and 800 volts at 750rpm and 57kW, 518 amps, 110 volts @ 450rpm respectively. When two or more of these locos are coupled in multiple, only the trailing loco is able to supply current for train heat.

Fibreglass again features in the construction of these machines with a removable translucent panel in this material being located over the engine. The double skinned cab roofs are also moulded in fibreglass.

When running light or with unfitted stock, the locomotive's straight air brake is used but when working with fitted stock, the automatic airbrake valve, operating through a distributor valve provides either air or vacuum braking as required.

Additional Information

BRC&W works numbers – DEL 92-189
Wheel arrangement – Bo-Bo
Engine – Sulzer 8LDA28A
B.H.P. – 1550 @ 750rpm
Weight in working order – 76 tons 9cwt,
    76tons 5cwt (Hastings)

Wheel diameter – 3ft 7ins
Control Equipment – Allen West
Length over buffers – 50ft 9ins
Height – 12ft 8ins
Overall width – 9ft 3ins, (D6586-97) 8ft 8ins
Top speed – 80mph
Maximum tractive effort – 45,000lbs

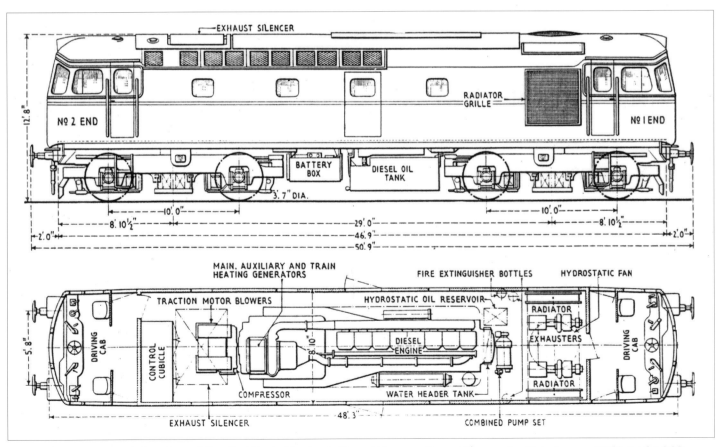

General arrangement drawing of the Southern Region's Type 3 locomotives. 98 were built between 1959 and 1962.

D6508 and D6509 stand outside the Birmingham Railway Carriage & Wagon Company's works at Smethwick prior to delivery to the Southern in April 1960.

The final 69 production diesel-electric locomotives to be constructed by BRC&W were built for service on the London Midland, North Eastern and Scottish Regions, although like their other BRC&W Type 2 predecessors they migrated to Scotland for the majority of their service. Numbered D5347 to D5415, they were delivered during 1961 and 1962 and incorporated a higher powered version of the Sulzer 6LDA28 engine, the 'B' type, rated at 1250hp. The extra power was achieved by intercooling, with the cooler being incorporated into the water circuit.

These locos later became class 27 in the revised order of things, but unlike their class 26 stablemates had roof mounted four character headcodes as well as several other detail differences.

The GEC WT 981 main generator, bolted to the crankshaft flange, comprised a 10 pole single bearing machine with four field windings – separately excited, self excited, reverse series and starting. It was continuously rated at 805kW, 1940 amps and 414 volts at 750rpm, while the GEC type WT782 auxiliary generator was a 6 pole machine rated at 57kW and 110 volts. The four GEC type WT459 traction motors were force ventilated 4 pole machines continuously rated at 236hp, 485 amps and 415 volts and connected in parallel across the main generator.

Fibreglass mouldings were included in the construction of these locomotives in the same way as were featured on the previous diesel-electric types. Where fitted, these machines had Stone-Vapor steam heating boilers for use when hauling passenger trains. D5370-78 were built specifically for freight duties and as such were not equipped with heating boilers. Up to three of these locomotives could be worked together in multiple and the braking equipment was the same as that fitted to D5300-46.

Additional Information
BRC&W works numbers – DEL 190 - DEL 258
Wheel Arrangement – Bo-Bo
Engine – Sulzer 6LDA28B
B.H.P – 1250 @ 750rpm
Weght in working order – 73.5 tons (with boiler),
    71 tons (without boiler)

Electrical equipment – G.E.C
Overall length – 50ft 9ins
Height – 12ft 8ins
Overall width – 9ft 3ins
Wheel diameter – 3ft 7ins
Top speed – 90mph
Maximum tractive effort – 40,000lbs

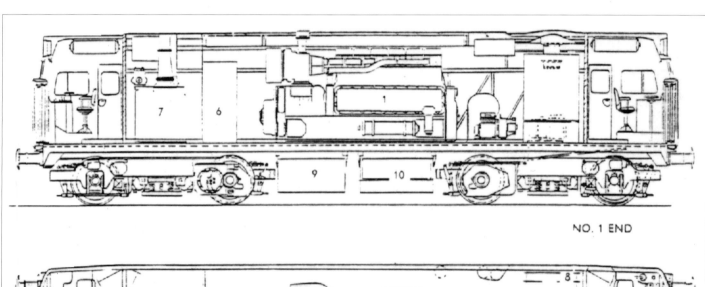

NO. 1 END

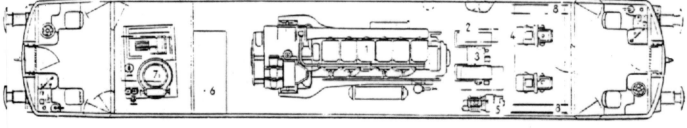

General arrangement :

1, Sulzer engine; 2, traction motor blowers; 3, combined pump set; 4, exhausters; 5, compressor;
6, control cubicle; 7, Stone-Vapor steam generator; 8, radiators; 9, water tank; 10, batteries.

Later to become class 27, sixty nine 1250hp Type 2s were built by BRC&W during 1961 and 1962. This drawing shows the internal layout of these locos.

CHAPTER 7

The White *LION*

With Type 4 orders in mind from British Railways, design work commenced on prototype diesel-electric *LION* around 1959 and resplendent in its white livery, D0260 was completed in April 1962. Its gold numbers were inspired by its works number, DEL 260, which followed on from those allocated to British Railways Type 2 locos (later class 27) which were in-build at that time. Particular attention had been paid to keeping *LION*'s weight to the absolute minimum and as a result, the specified maximum axle load requirement of 19 tons was achieved on six axles rather than eight. Revised Type 4 engine power requirements, calling for a minimum traction output of 2500hp and a further 250hp for ETH, were met by Sulzer with their new 12LDA28-C pressure charged engine. Similar to the B type, it was uprated by improving the intercooling system and raising the crankshaft speed from 750rpm to 800rpm at full load. Indeed, at the time of building it was said to be the most powerful rail-traction diesel engine in Western Europe. Although designed with a top service speed of 100mph, it is reported that this was comfortably exceeded while on trial.

Many new and innovative features were built into *LION*, one of which was the extensive use of rubber in the suspension system to improve the riding quality. Dual train heating was also provided in the shape of a Spanner Mk111B oil-fired boiler together with an AEI AG 106, 800 volt electric train heating generator.

A translucent fibreglass roof trap located over the engine, which could be raised pneumatically six inches, was incorporated to allow heat from the engine room to dispel quicker and provide a cooler environment for fitters needing to carry out in-service repairs. Radiators and air filters were roof mounted to reduce their vulnerability to dirt and contamination, while at the same time simplifying the design of the load-bearing bodyside members by eliminating the large apertures which otherwise may have been necessary. The addition of fluting below waist level gave *LION* a pleasing finishing touch and enhanced its clean lines.

LION was fitted with Westinghouse vacuum controlled air brakes and vacuum train braking, although for light running or when hauling unfitted stock, the locomotive's straight air brake was used. The generator group comprised three AEI machines which included a 384kW, 800 volt type AG106 for train heat, a 780 volt type TG5303 for traction and a 110 volt type AG105 for auxiliaries. Patented features were built into the traction generator which reduced the amount of copper required for the windings. This gave a significant weight saving which allowed a larger diameter and shorter armature to be incorporated. Traction was provided by six AEI type 253 motors, one per axle, which were axle-hung, nose suspended and force ventilated.

During 1961 and the early part of this year, we have in conjunction with Associated Electrical Industries and Sulzer Brothers, built the prototype of a new and improved design of locomotive of 2750 horse power which we are submitting to the British Transport Commission for inspection and test. This prototype was available to support our tender for type 4 locomotives which was in the hands of the Commission on 16 May 1962 and must be considered to be among the best available in the world. We understand we are the only British manufacturers who are supporting their tender with a fully operating prototype.

This extract from the Chairman's statement at the 1962 annual general meeting of BRC&W brought with it high hopes that orders for this new private venture locomotive, built to the revised Type 4 specification, would be forthcoming. Quarter of a million pounds was spent in building the *LION* which had been painstakingly produced as a technically advanced top class locomotive upon which BRC&W's fortunes were firmly pinned. Its first outing was a works test between Birmingham and Shrewsbury and *LION*'s official debut on British Railways was made during May 1962. Following a civic send-off from Smethwick on the 25th, it was placed on show at Marylebone station three days later. During early tests with passenger stock, it conquered the Lickey incline unaided and its ultimate achievement was to haul 20 coaches up the 1 in 38 gradient from a standing start which it did with relish and without a banker.

Regrettably, no orders materialised either from British Railways or from any of the overseas railways and *LION* quietly slipped into oblivion. Withdrawal came in October 1963 after just 18 months, and during early 1965 it made its last journey to South Yorkshire to be broken up.

Additional Data

Wheel arrangement – Co-Co
Wheel diameter – 3ft 9ins
Overall length – 63ft 6ins
Fuel capacity – 850 gallons
Width over body – 8ft 10ins
Weight in working order – 114 tons
Height – 12ft 9ins
Maximum tractive effort – 55,000lbs

Right: LION being strain gauged whilst under loaded conditions. A 200 ton end loading has also been applied.

Below: LION whilst under construction at Smethwick. It is seen undergoing strain testing.

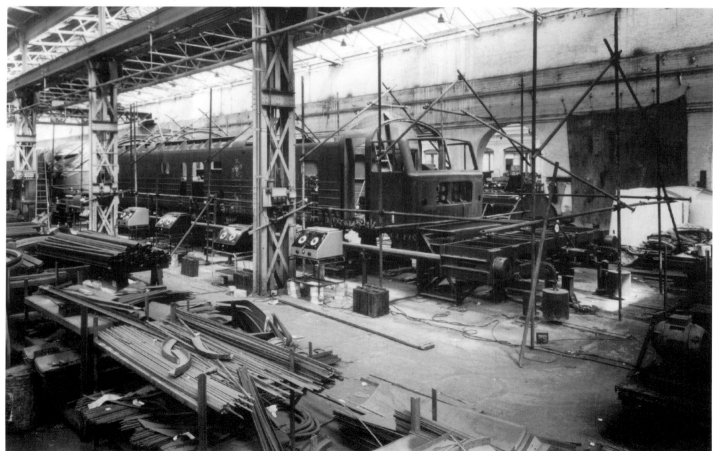

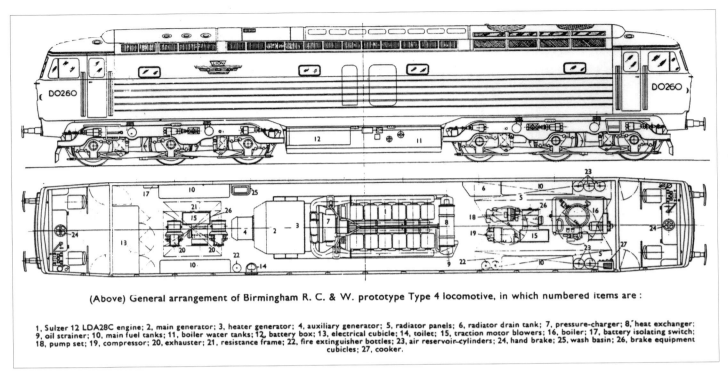

(Above) General arrangement of Birmingham R. C. & W. prototype Type 4 locomotive, in which numbered items are :

1, Sulzer 12 LDA28C engine; 2, main generator; 3, heater generator; 4, auxiliary generator; 5, radiator panels; 6, radiator drain tank; 7, pressure-charger; 8, heat exchanger; 9, oil strainer; 10, main fuel tanks; 11, boiler water tanks; 12, battery box; 13, electrical cubicle; 14, toilet; 15, traction motor blowers; 16, boiler; 17, battery isolating switch; 18, pump set; 19, compressor; 20, exhauster; 21, resistance frame; 22, fire extinguisher bottles; 23, air reservoir cylinders; 24, hand brake; 25, wash basin; 26, brake equipment cubicles; 27, cooker.

General arrangement drawing of *LION.*

LION during one of its test runs.

CHAPTER 8

Decline and Closure

Following the war, output and profitability was on the increase and by 1950 the company was in a buoyant position. It was however, becoming apparent during the early 1950s that rolling stock production was joining a shrinking market and the effects of over-capacity in the industry were beginning to emerge. This was due in part to the ability of British Railways to build a significant proportion of its own rolling stock in-house, with consequentially fewer orders coming from those quarters.

BRC&W's traditional overseas markets were also looking closer to home for their stock and what orders there were, were subject to the severest of competition. Rises in wage rates and steadily increasing costs were paring profit margins to the bone. Peaks and troughs in production came in rapid succession and it was essential that a niche in the market was found to bring about some stability – for a while at least.

With steam traction disappearing, world-wide railway modernisation was starting to gain momentum. The diesel market was just the niche the company was looking for and orders were secured initially with overseas railways for locomotives and railcars. These were followed in the mid and late 1950s by orders from British Railways for diesel-electric and AC electric locomotives as well as for diesel multiple units. Many of these were built in collaboration with other manufacturers and the decision to enter this market was, indeed, a shrewd one. Orders for carriages and wagons alone would have been insufficient to sustain production for very long.

Indeed, it was reported at the 1960 AGM in respect of 1959, that the sales value of locomotives exceeded those for all other work put together. The picture at that time showed locomotive orders in-hand were sufficient to keep those shops busy until early 1962 and orders for coaches until 1961. Wagon production, however, was at an all time low with no visible signs of improvement.

In 1960 the company was awarded a contract to build 338 driving motor cars and 112 non-driving motor cars for London Transport's underground system. The following year the company asked to be relieved of this work as it would have involved them in heavy losses. Following negotiations and the setting of a penalty payment, this order went to Metro-Cammell. Such were the times that it would actually have cost more to produce stock, than not.

In general terms, the trend of reduced work from both home and overseas, coupled with over-capacity in the industry was continuing. To this was added the unwelcome ingredient of increasing costs. As far as overseas orders were concerned, foreign competitors were able to offer extended terms of credit which British manufacturers at that time could not. This put us at a major disadvantage. By 1962, home orders had virtually disappeared, but it was essential to have a reasonable domestic turnover to compete effectively on the world market. However, this was not the case, nor likely to be. Diversification seemed the only logical way ahead. By this time, such work as there was, was carried out in the South Works by a few hundred workers. It was anticipated that the capacity there would be more than enough to satisfy any potential orders. The North Works, which comprised about one third of the covered floor space had been vacated and cleared for either disposal or lease.

In January 1963 the chairman held out very little hope of any new orders coming from British Railways, who themselves had a large manufacturing capability. All the main contracts had been completed and despite tendering for new work, the company had been unsuccessful in gaining any more orders. Many more workers by this time had either left or been made redundant. Taking all the circumstances into account, BRC&W reluctantly decided to cease the manufacture of rolling stock and locomotives and close down the works. By renting-out their large industrial area to other concerns, it was also hoped that former company employees would be able to find alternative work on site.

Closure at the beginning of 1963 marked the end of a long and distinguished history of producing wagons, carriages, railcars, buses, locomotives, tanks and aircraft. Many writers have stated that BRC&W went bankrupt, owing hundreds of thousands of pounds to creditors. Nothing could be further from the truth. Indeed, a profit of over £370,000 had been made in 1962 and a dividend of 10% paid! The company had examined its options very carefully and decided to make the best of the assets it already had. This was achieved by ceasing production, letting-out the factory space and ground to other businesses and securing an income from rentals.

The BRC&W was re-named The Birmingham Wagon Company (shades of 1854!) in September 1963 and this new holding company developed new business interests in property development, hire purchase, property investment and industrial and merchant banking.

Examples of Builders' plates

An example of a BRC&W owner's plate as carried on the wagon rental fleet.

Maker's plate from a London, Tilbury & Southend Railway carriage.

Maker's plate from a vehicle exported to Argentina.

Shunting locomotives at BRC&W.

The following is a list of locomotives used on the works internal railway system. All were standard gauge.

Running No.	Type	Maker	Maker's No.	Date Built	Remarks
2	0-4-0 Crane Tank	Hawthorn Leslie	2446	1900	Sold/scrapped
No.19	0-4-0 Saddle Tank	Hawthorn Leslie	2714	1907	Scrapped c.1951
No.28	0-4-0 Saddle Tank	Hawthorn Leslie	3283	1917	Scrapped c.1951
No.11	0-4-0 Saddle Tank	Avonside Engine	1830	1919	Sold in 1952
	6w Diesel Electric	Crompton Parkinson/ Andrew Barclay	101 367	1945 1945	On loan 1945/46
	0-4-0 Diesel Mechanical	John Fowler	4210009	1949	Sold in 1963
	0-4-0 Diesel Mechanical	Rbt Stephenson & Hawthorns	6989	1940	Sold in 1963

In addition, there was probably at least one locomotive here prior to 1900.

This information has been supplied by courtesy of the Industrial Railway Society, see their Handbook WM, *Industrial Locomotives of West Midlands.*

'Modified Hall' No. 6975 heads a special traffic movement from BRC&W to Avonmouth Docks on 14 January 1951, hauling an Egyptian State Railways 5 car diesel unit. Seen at Hatherley, Cheltenham, progress is rather more sedate than the 93mph achieved by one of the units on a trial run a month earlier between Smethwick and Aynho.   PHOTO: W. DENDY